Originally launched on Facebook, Rupert Fawcett's brilliantly observed, touchingly truthful Off The Leash cartoons have developed a huge daily following around the world.

His books *Off The Leash: The Secret Life of Dogs* and now *Off The Leash: A Dog's Best Friend* bring together the very best of those cartoons, featuring the secret thoughts and conversations of dogs of every size, shape and breed. They are a celebration of our favourite belly-scratching, tail-chasing, bed-stealing canine friends — for dog lovers everywhere.

Also by Rupert Fawcett

Off The Leash: The Secret Life of Dogs

Off The Leash

A DOG'S BEST FRIEND

Rupert Fawcett

BOXTREE

First published 2014 by Boxtree
an imprint of Pan Macmillan, a division of Macmillan Publishers Limited
Pan Macmillan, 20 New Wharf Road, London N1 9RR
Basingstoke and Oxford
Associated companies throughout the world
www.panmacmillan.com

ISBN 978-1-4472-6808-6

1 3 5 7 9 8 6 4 2

A CIP catalogue record for this book is available from the British Library.

Printed and bound in China

Visit **www.panmacmillan.com** to read more about all our books
and to buy them. You will also find features, author interviews and
news of any author events, and you can sign up for e-newsletters
so that you're always first to hear about our new releases.

Foreword

When I started posting daily dog cartoons on Facebook in March 2012 I had no idea they would become so popular. Off The Leash now has fans all over the world and my first book *The Secret Life of Dogs* is being translated into several languages. I receive huge numbers of messages from dog owners around the globe, and also many from people who don't have any pets at all, and what constantly strikes me is the enormous love we all have for our four-legged friends. Not only do we love them with a passion but we often find them extremely funny too, as dogs can be so comical in so many different ways. Alongside the usual cartoons, *A Dog's Best Friend* includes new pencil drawings of dogs and their owners, reflecting the special relationships we have with our friends. I hope you will find some of that love and humour reflected in this book.

Rupert Fawcett

For Howard, Melissa and Isabelle

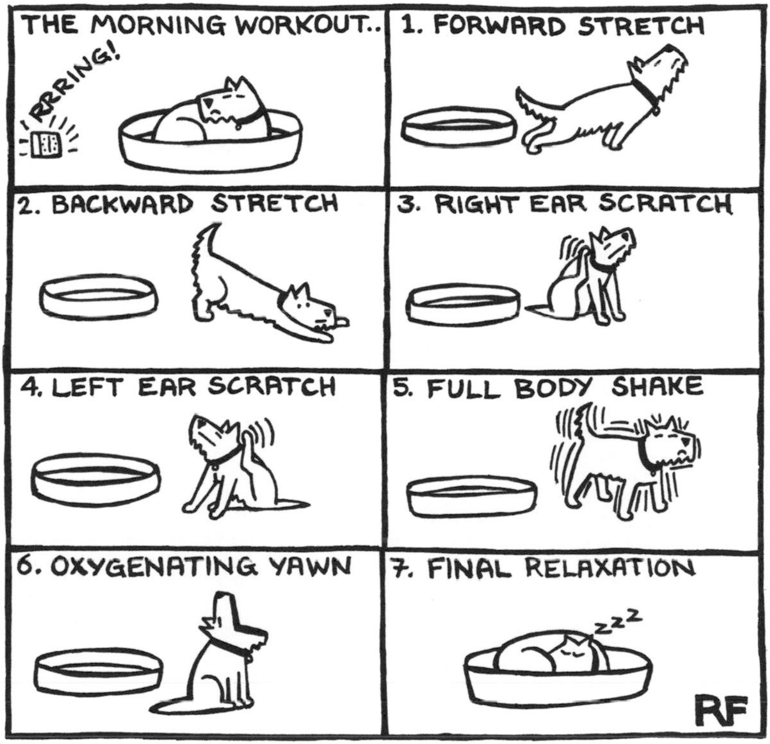
THE MORNING WORKOUT..
RRRING!
1. FORWARD STRETCH
2. BACKWARD STRETCH
3. RIGHT EAR SCRATCH
4. LEFT EAR SCRATCH
5. FULL BODY SHAKE
6. OXYGENATING YAWN
7. FINAL RELAXATION
zzz
RF

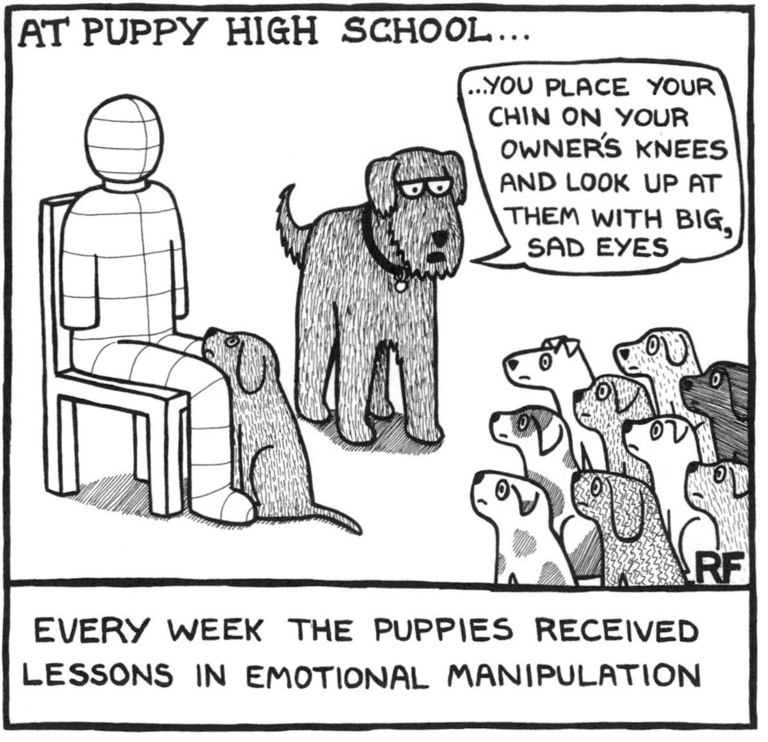
AT PUPPY HIGH SCHOOL...
...YOU PLACE YOUR CHIN ON YOUR OWNER'S KNEES AND LOOK UP AT THEM WITH BIG, SAD EYES
RF

EVERY WEEK THE PUPPIES RECEIVED LESSONS IN EMOTIONAL MANIPULATION

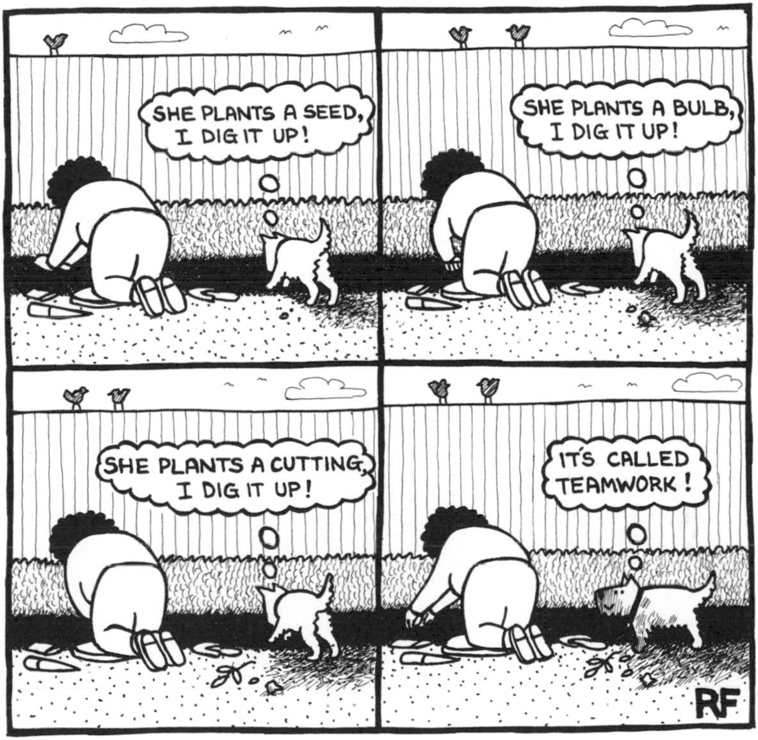
SHE PLANTS A SEED, I DIG IT UP!
SHE PLANTS A BULB, I DIG IT UP!
SHE PLANTS A CUTTING, I DIG IT UP!
IT'S CALLED TEAMWORK!
RF

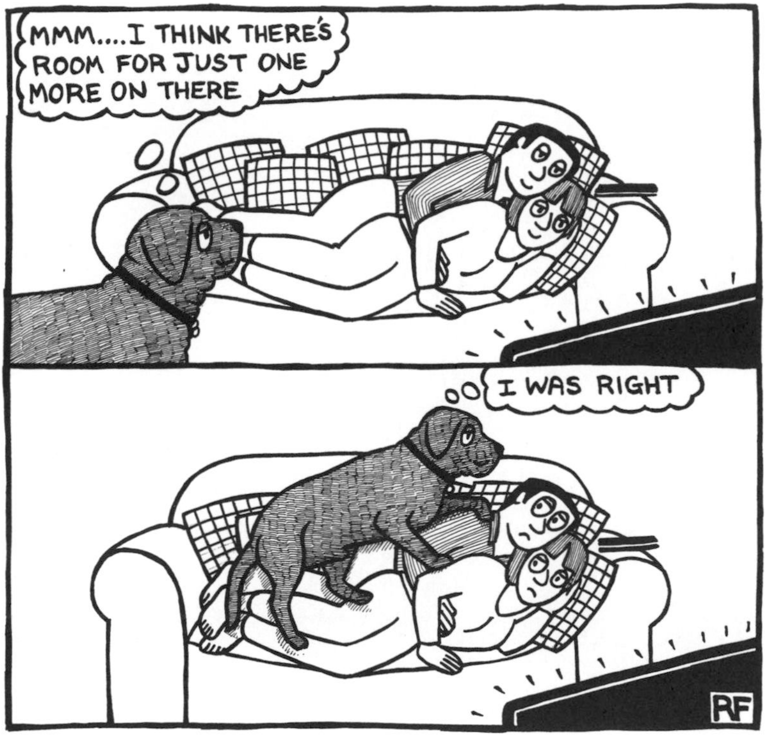
MMM....I THINK THERE'S ROOM FOR JUST ONE MORE ON THERE
I WAS RIGHT
RF

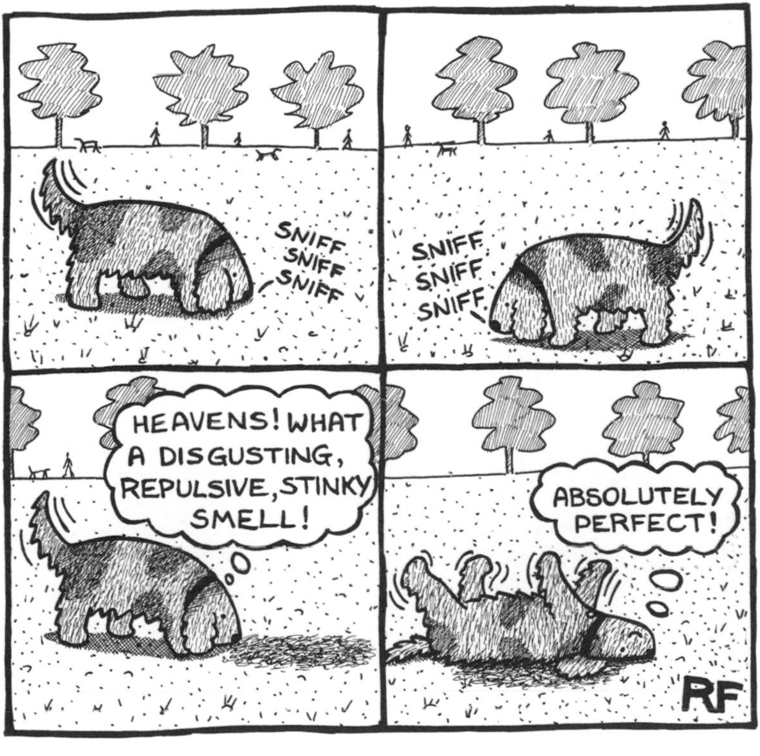
SNIFF
SNIFF
SNIFF
SNIFF
SNIFF
SNIFF
HEAVENS! WHAT A DISGUSTING, REPULSIVE, STINKY SMELL!
ABSOLUTELY PERFECT!
RF

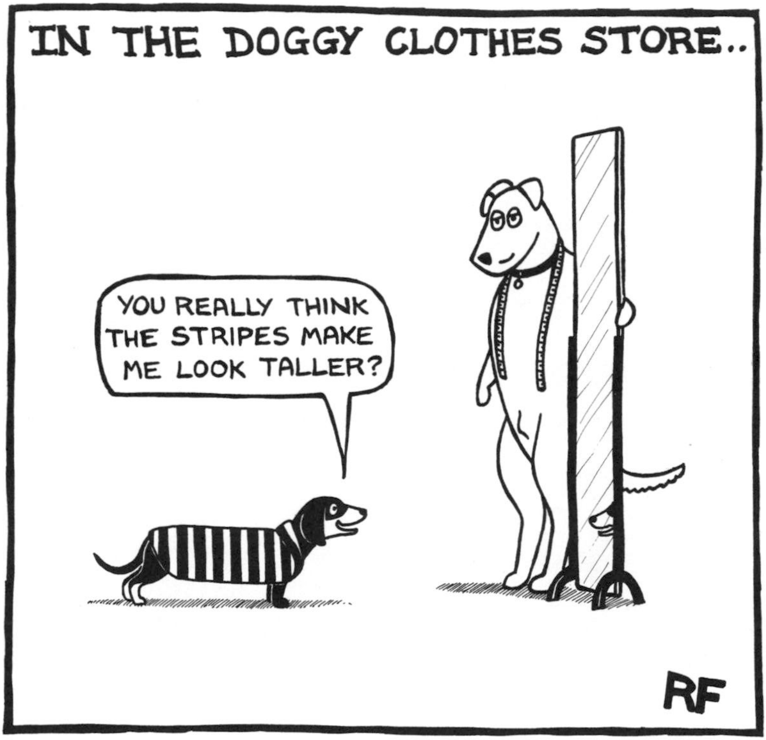
IN THE DOGGY CLOTHES STORE..
YOU REALLY THINK THE STRIPES MAKE ME LOOK TALLER?
RF

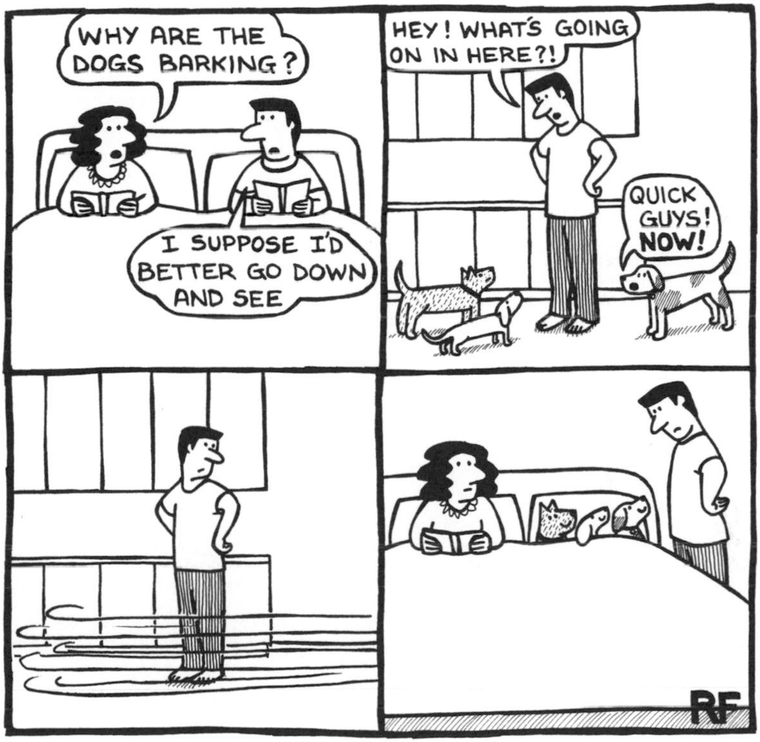
WHY ARE THE DOGS BARKING?
I SUPPOSE I'D BETTER GO DOWN AND SEE
HEY! WHAT'S GOING ON IN HERE?!
QUICK GUYS! NOW!
RF

THE SUNBATHERS

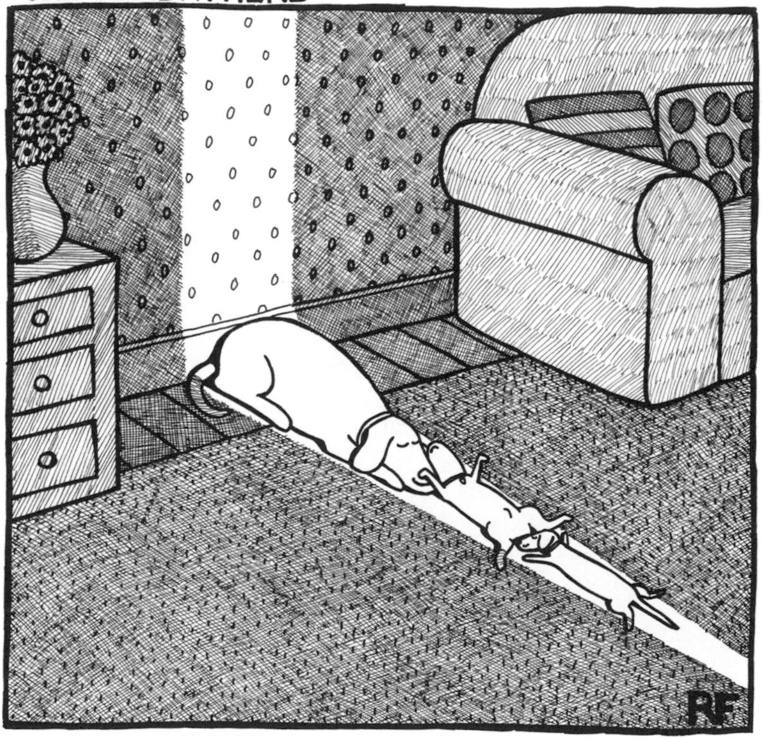
RF

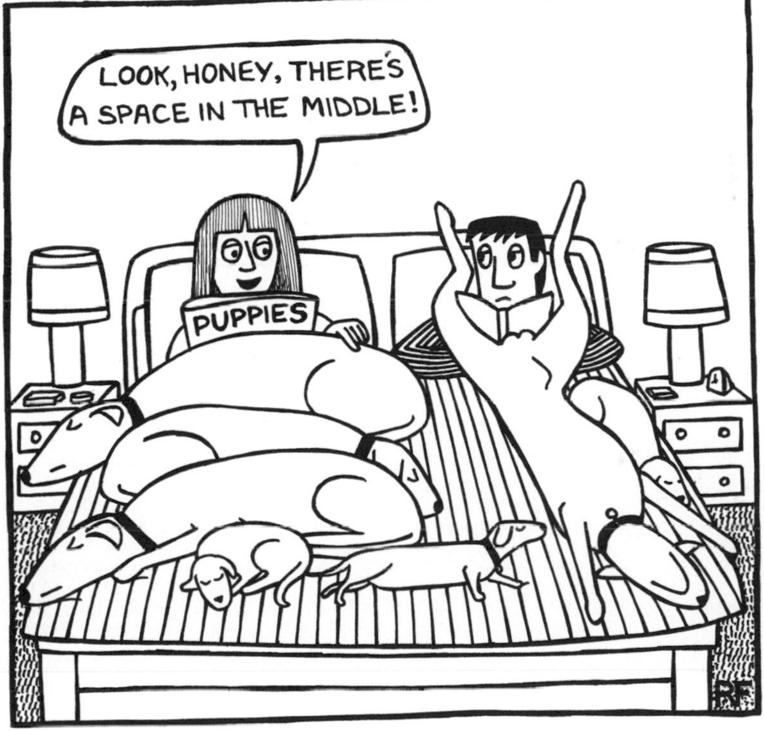
LOOK, HONEY, THERE'S A SPACE IN THE MIDDLE!
PUPPIES
RF

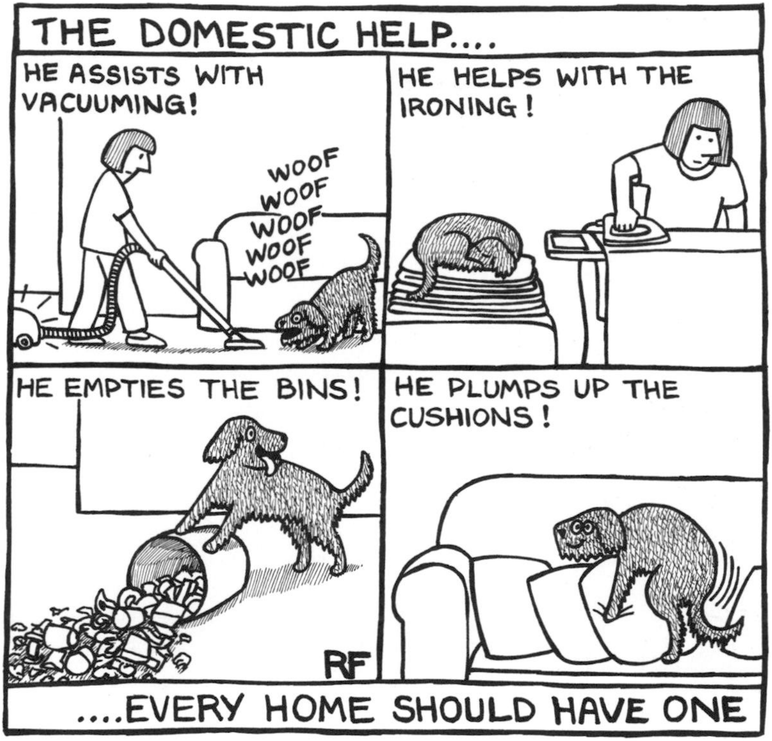
THE DOMESTIC HELP....
HE ASSISTS WITH VACUUMING!
WOOF WOOF WOOF WOOF WOOF
HE HELPS WITH THE IRONING!
HE EMPTIES THE BINS!
RF
HE PLUMPS UP THE CUSHIONS!
....EVERY HOME SHOULD HAVE ONE

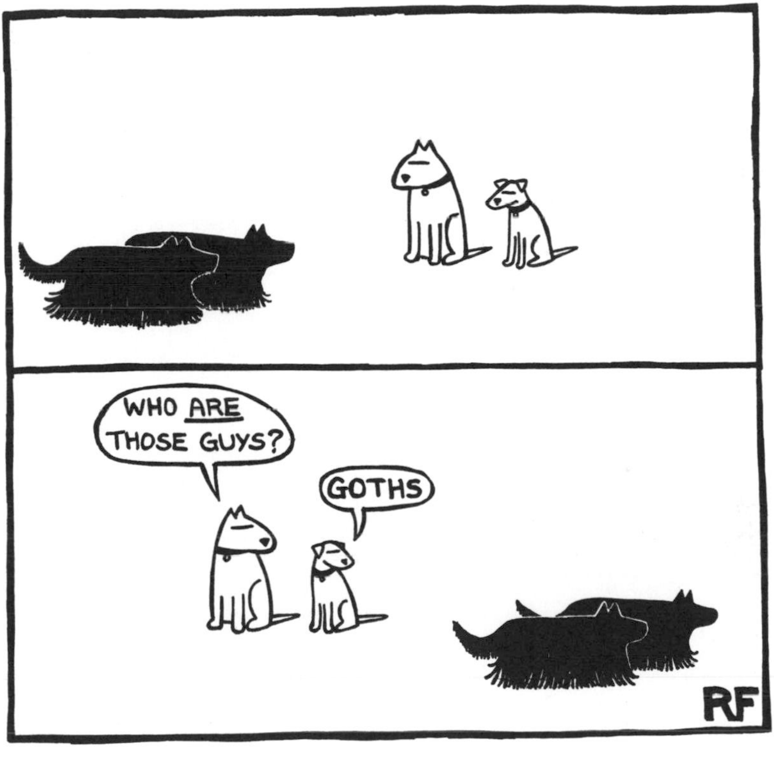
WHO ARE THOSE GUYS?
GOTHS
RF

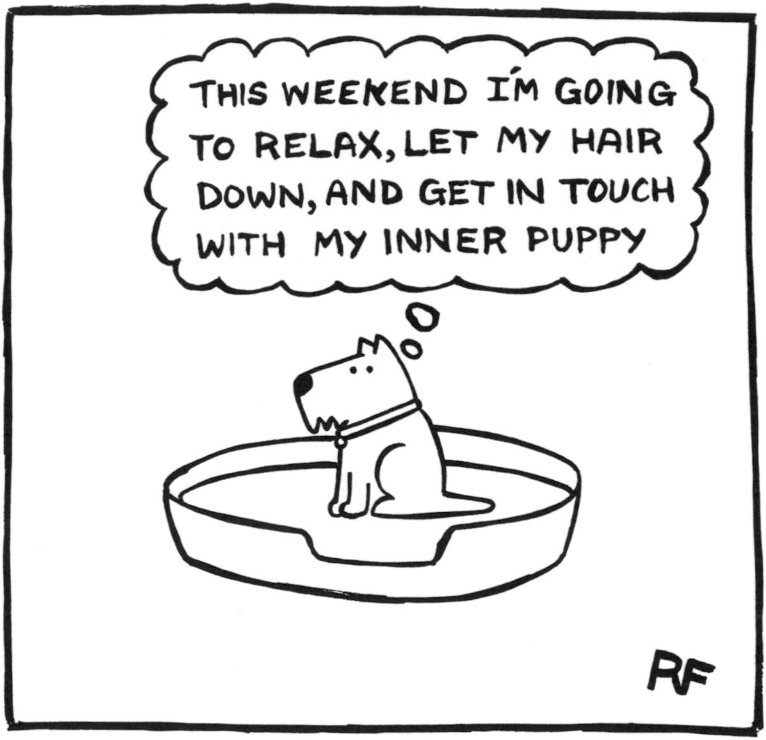
THIS WEEKEND I'M GOING TO RELAX, LET MY HAIR DOWN, AND GET IN TOUCH WITH MY INNER PUPPY
RF

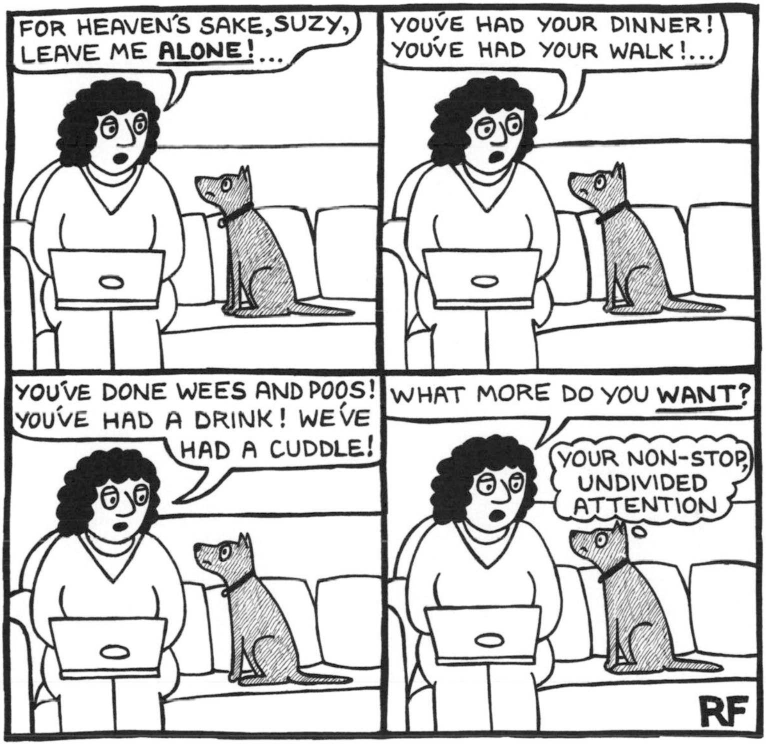
FOR HEAVEN'S SAKE, SUZY, LEAVE ME ALONE!...
YOU'VE HAD YOUR DINNER! YOU'VE HAD YOUR WALK!...
YOU'VE DONE WEES AND POOS! YOU'VE HAD A DRINK! WE'VE HAD A CUDDLE!
WHAT MORE DO YOU WANT?
YOUR NON-STOP, UNDIVIDED ATTENTION
RF

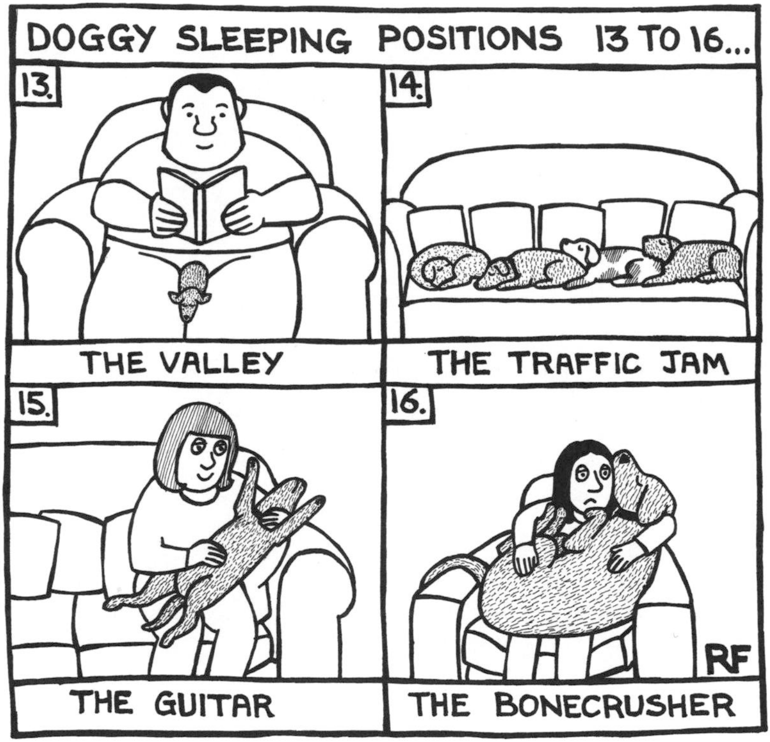
DOGGY SLEEPING POSITIONS 13 TO 16...
13.
THE VALLEY
14.
THE TRAFFIC JAM
15.
THE GUITAR
16.
RF
THE BONECRUSHER

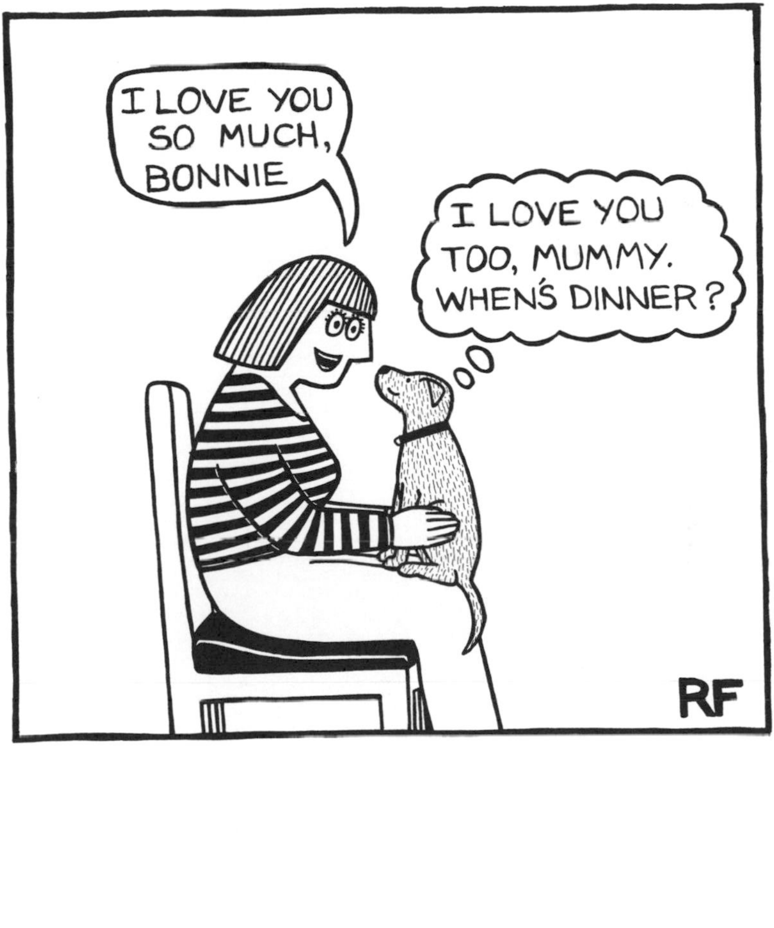
I LOVE YOU SO MUCH, BONNIE
I LOVE YOU TOO, MUMMY. WHEN'S DINNER?
RF

AT THE DOGGY LIBRARY...

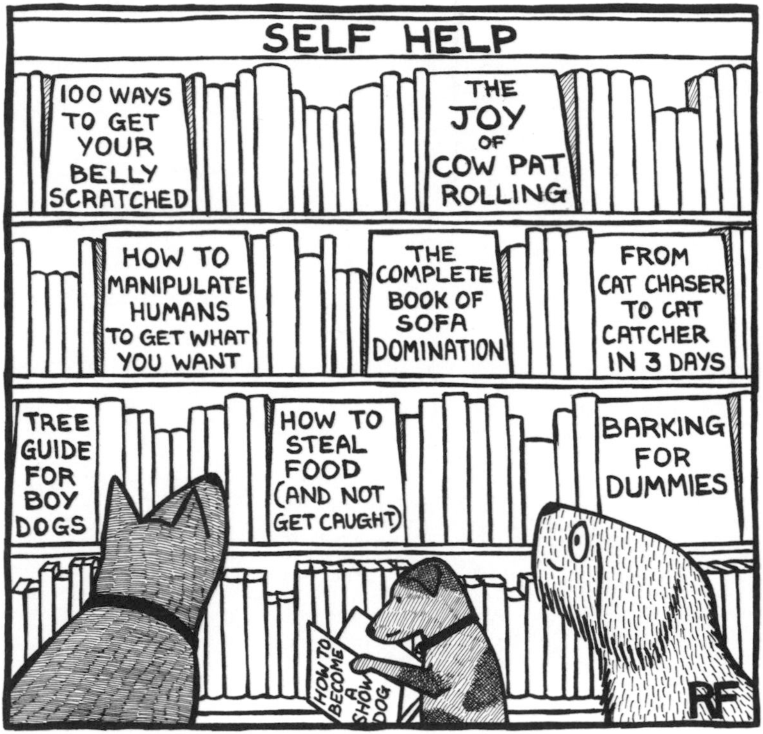

SELF HELP
100 WAYS TO GET YOUR BELLY SCRATCHED
THE JOY OF COW PAT ROLLING
HOW TO MANIPULATE HUMANS TO GET WHAT YOU WANT
THE COMPLETE BOOK OF SOFA DOMINATION
FROM CAT CHASER TO CAT CATCHER IN 3 DAYS
TREE GUIDE FOR BOY DOGS
HOW TO STEAL FOOD (AND NOT GET CAUGHT)
BARKING FOR DUMMIES
HOW TO BECOME A SHOW DOG
RF

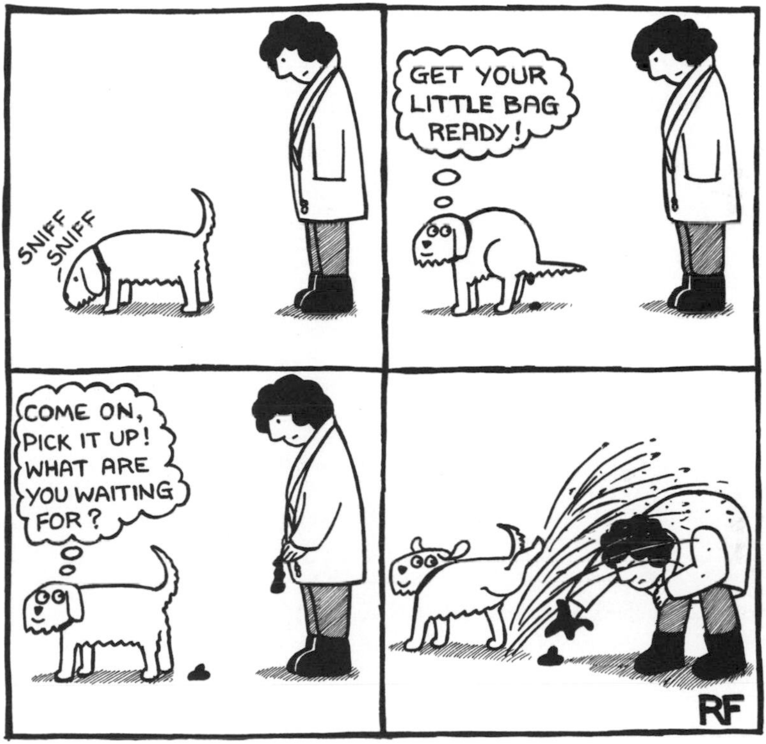
SNIFF SNIFF
GET YOUR LITTLE BAG READY!
COME ON, PICK IT UP! WHAT ARE YOU WAITING FOR?
RF

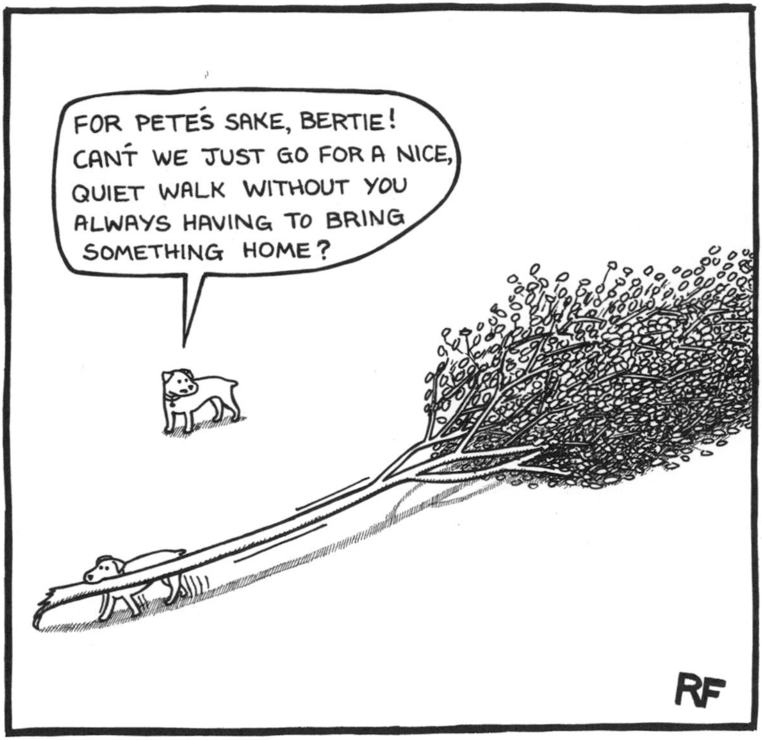
FOR PETE'S SAKE, BERTIE! CAN'T WE JUST GO FOR A NICE, QUIET WALK WITHOUT YOU ALWAYS HAVING TO BRING SOMETHING HOME?
RF

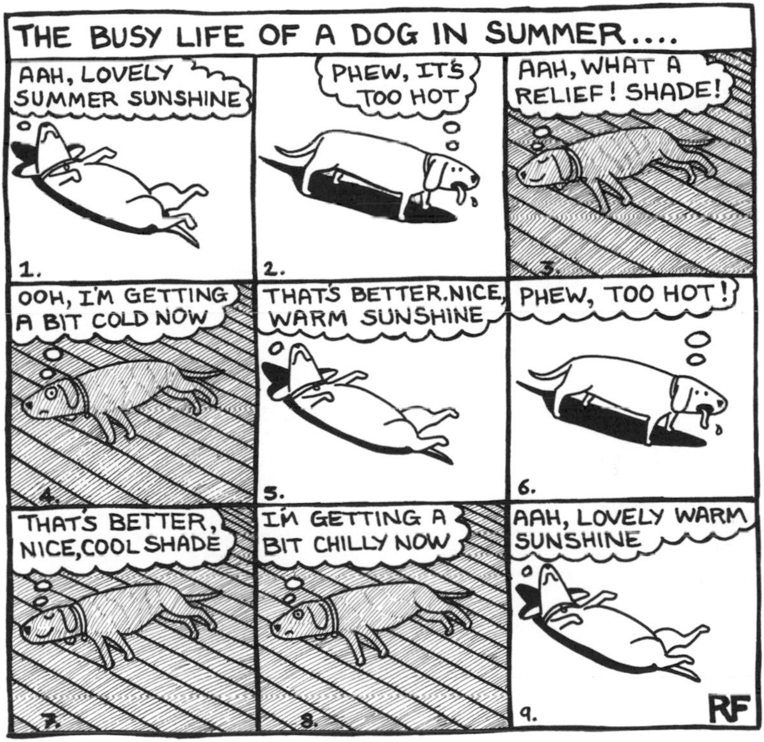
THE BUSY LIFE OF A DOG IN SUMMER....
AAH, LOVELY SUMMER SUNSHINE
1.
PHEW, IT'S TOO HOT
2.
AAH, WHAT A RELIEF! SHADE!
3.
OOH, I'M GETTING A BIT COLD NOW
4.
THAT'S BETTER. NICE, WARM SUNSHINE
5.
PHEW, TOO HOT!
6.
THAT'S BETTER, NICE, COOL SHADE
7.
I'M GETTING A BIT CHILLY NOW
8.
AAH, LOVELY WARM SUNSHINE
9.
RF

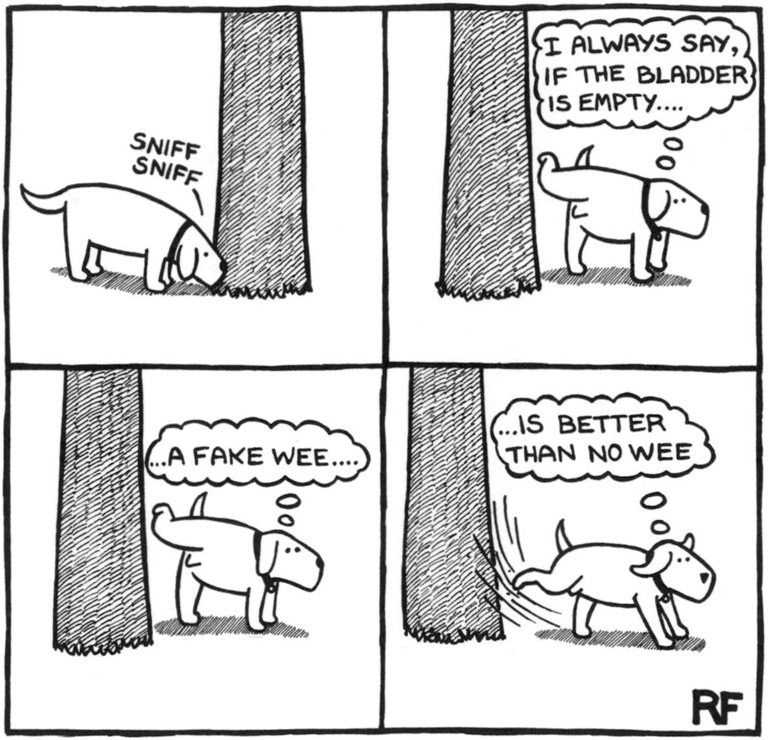
SNIFF
SNIFF
I ALWAYS SAY,
IF THE BLADDER
IS EMPTY....
...A FAKE WEE....
...IS BETTER
THAN NO WEE
RF

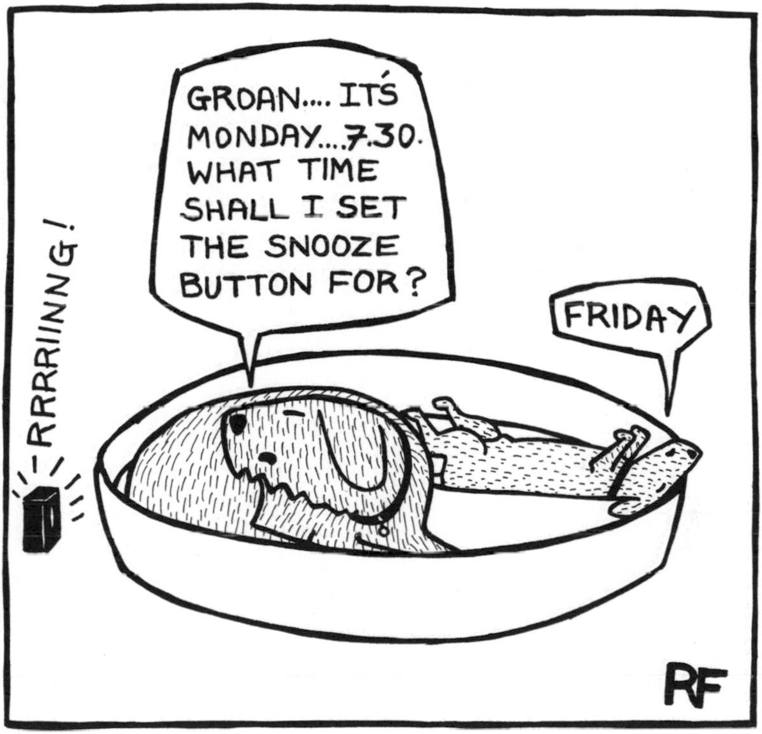
RRRRIINNG!
GROAN.... IT'S MONDAY....7.30. WHAT TIME SHALL I SET THE SNOOZE BUTTON FOR?
FRIDAY
RF

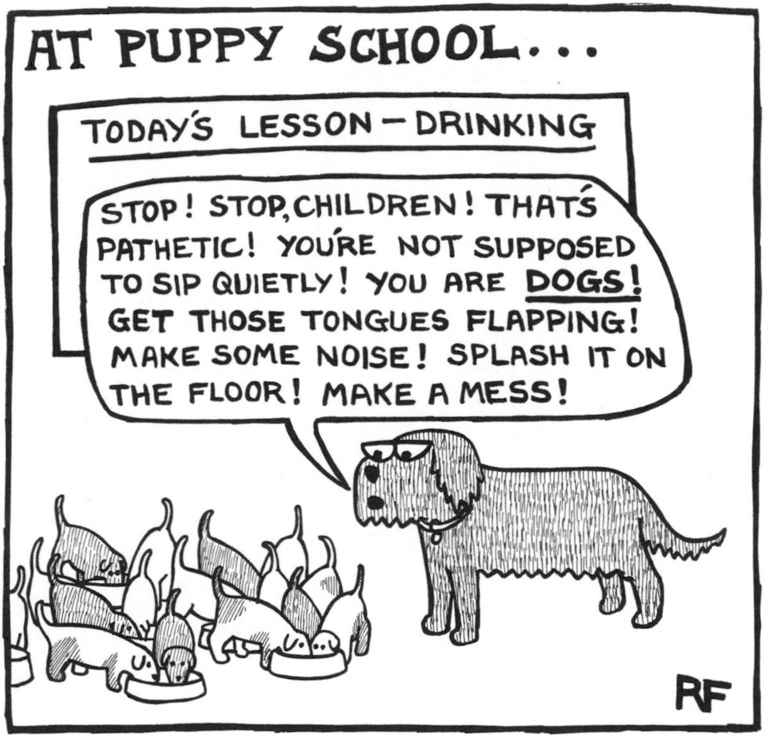

AT PUPPY SCHOOL...
TODAY'S LESSON – DRINKING
STOP! STOP, CHILDREN! THAT'S PATHETIC! YOU'RE NOT SUPPOSED TO SIP QUIETLY! YOU ARE DOGS! GET THOSE TONGUES FLAPPING! MAKE SOME NOISE! SPLASH IT ON THE FLOOR! MAKE A MESS!
RF

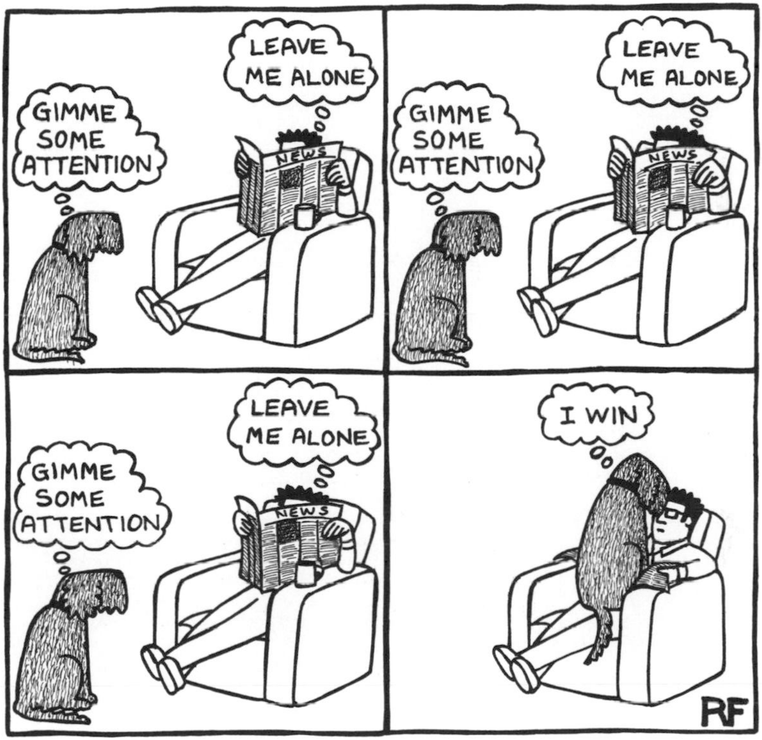
GIMME SOME ATTENTION
LEAVE ME ALONE
NEWS
GIMME SOME ATTENTION
LEAVE ME ALONE
NEWS
GIMME SOME ATTENTION
LEAVE ME ALONE
NEWS
I WIN
RF

A WINTER WALK

RF

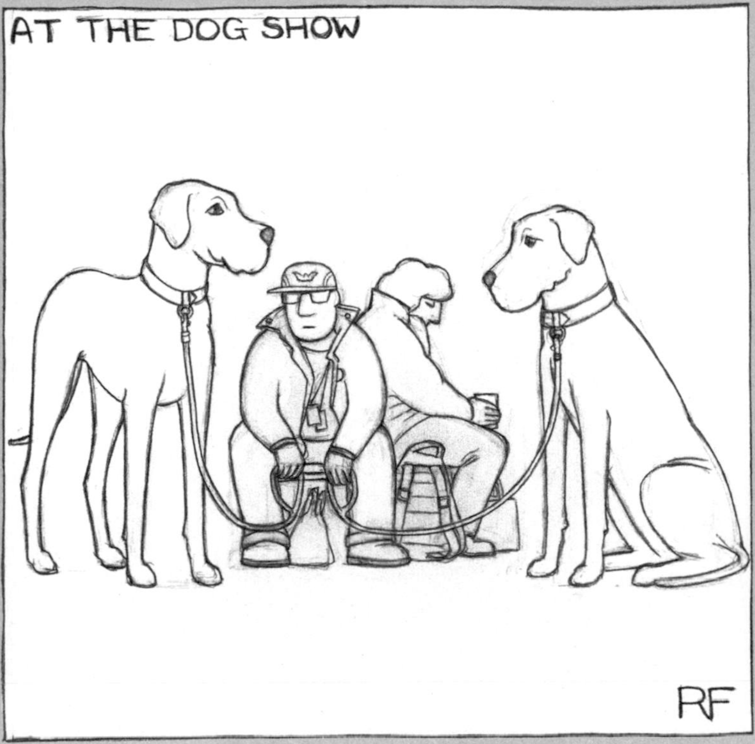
AT THE DOG SHOW
RF

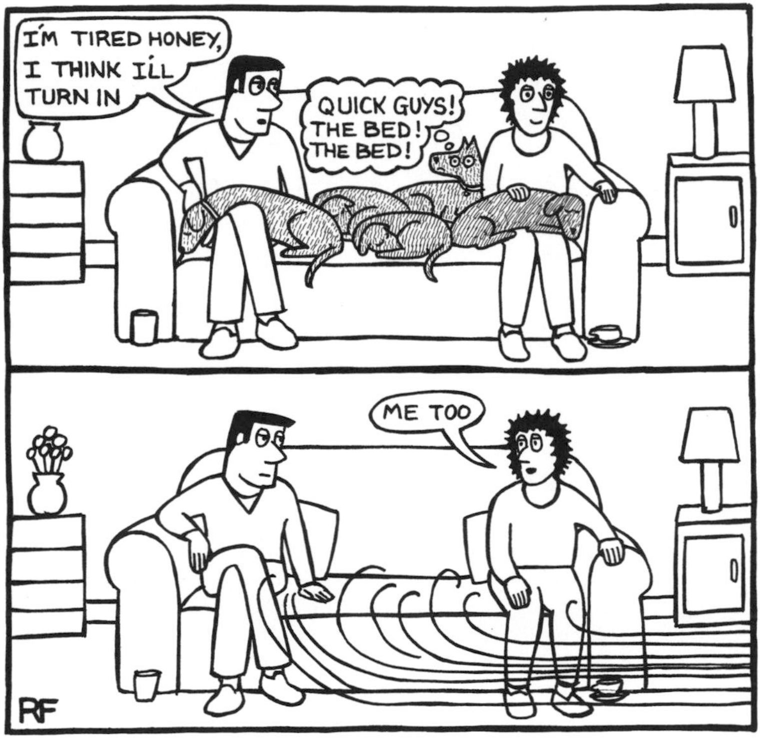
I'M TIRED HONEY, I THINK I'LL TURN IN
QUICK GUYS! THE BED! THE BED!
ME TOO
RF

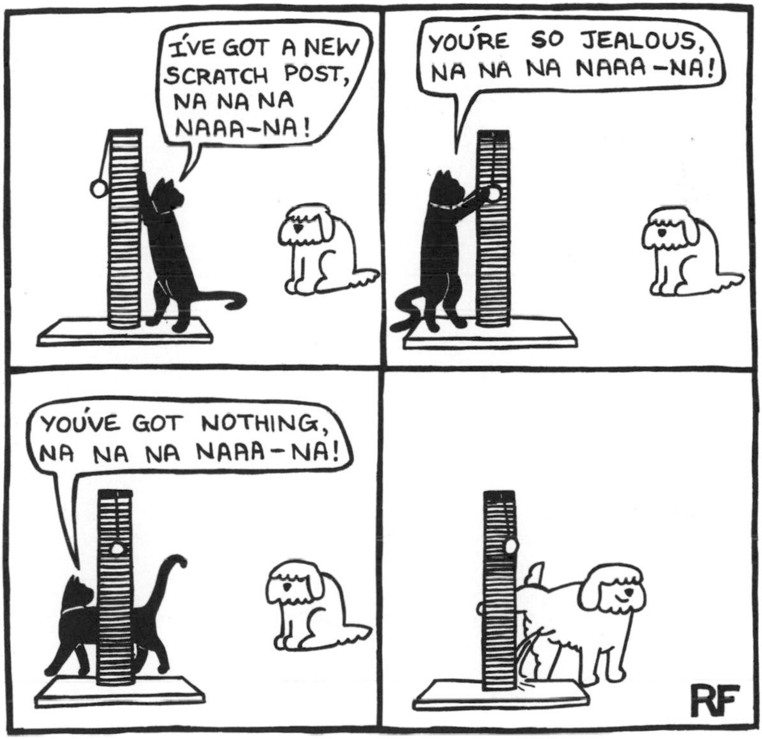
I'VE GOT A NEW SCRATCH POST, NA NA NA NAAA-NA!
YOU'RE SO JEALOUS, NA NA NA NAAA-NA!
YOU'VE GOT NOTHING, NA NA NA NAAA-NA!
RF

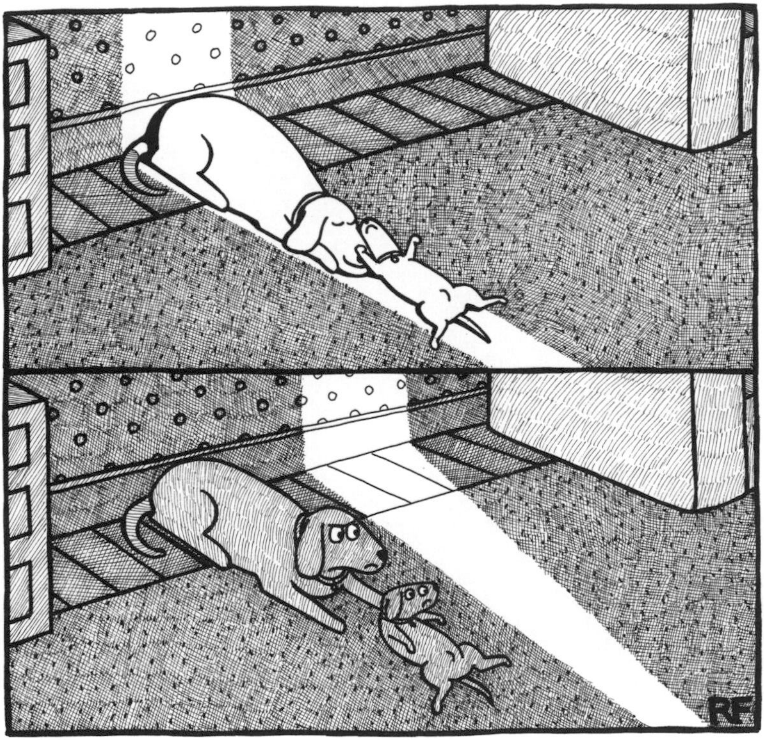
RF

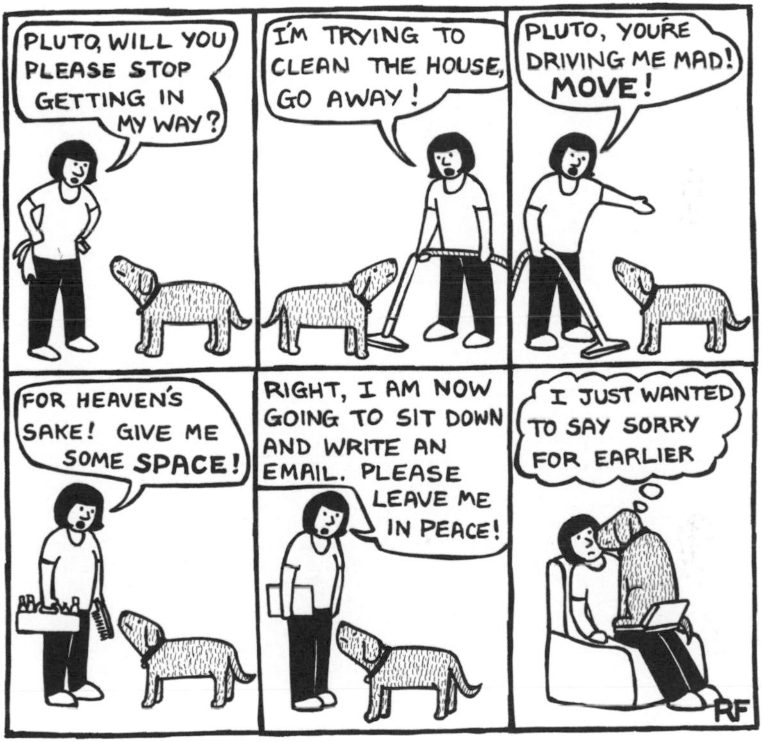
PLUTO, WILL YOU PLEASE STOP GETTING IN MY WAY?
I'M TRYING TO CLEAN THE HOUSE, GO AWAY!
PLUTO, YOU'RE DRIVING ME MAD! MOVE!
FOR HEAVEN'S SAKE! GIVE ME SOME SPACE!
RIGHT, I AM NOW GOING TO SIT DOWN AND WRITE AN EMAIL. PLEASE LEAVE ME IN PEACE!
I JUST WANTED TO SAY SORRY FOR EARLIER
RF

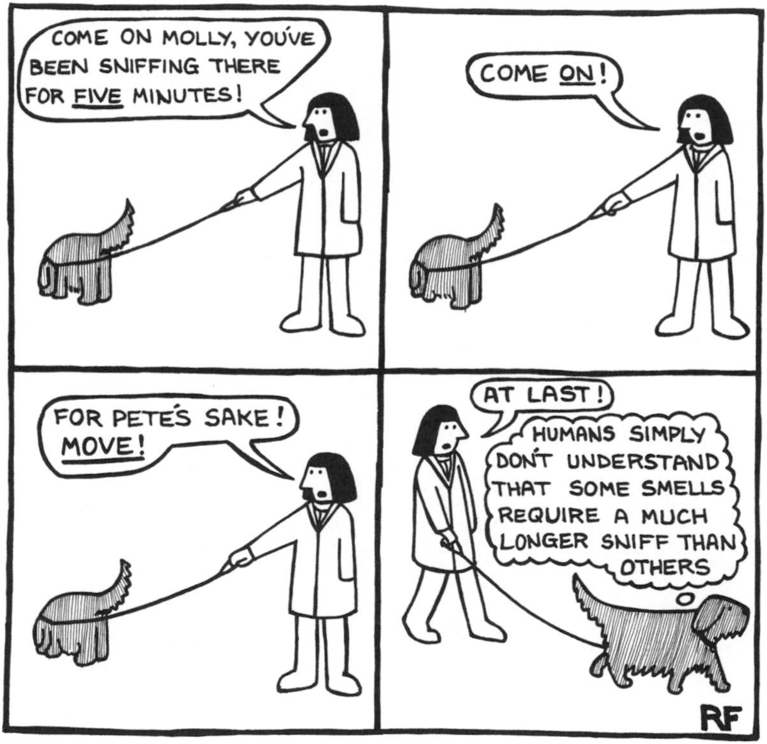
COME ON MOLLY, YOU'VE BEEN SNIFFING THERE FOR FIVE MINUTES!
COME ON!
FOR PETE'S SAKE! MOVE!
AT LAST!
HUMANS SIMPLY DON'T UNDERSTAND THAT SOME SMELLS REQUIRE A MUCH LONGER SNIFF THAN OTHERS
RF

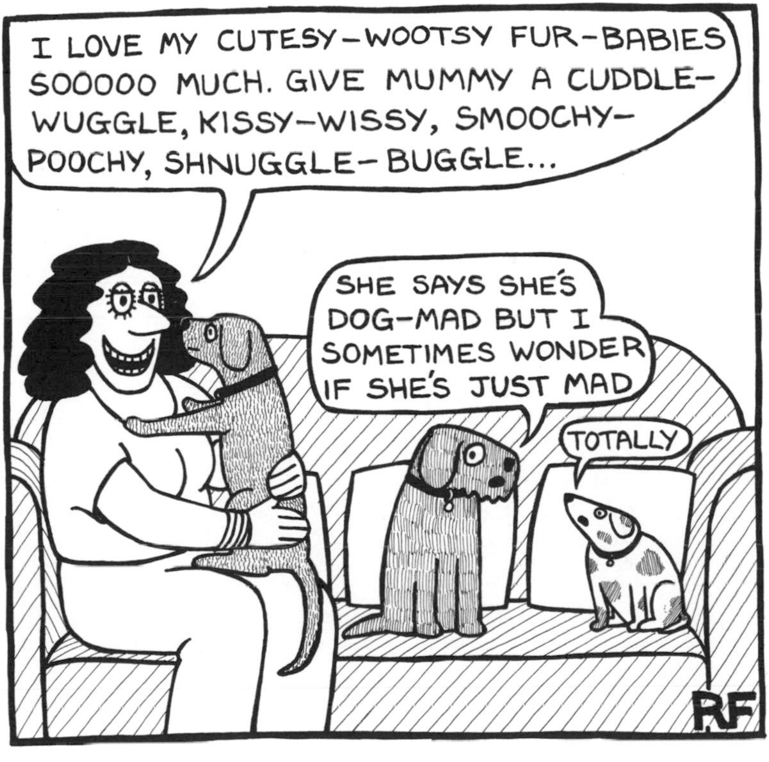
I LOVE MY CUTESY-WOOTSY FUR-BABIES SOOOOO MUCH. GIVE MUMMY A CUDDLE-WUGGLE, KISSY-WISSY, SMOOCHY-POOCHY, SHNUGGLE-BUGGLE...
SHE SAYS SHE'S DOG-MAD BUT I SOMETIMES WONDER IF SHE'S JUST MAD
TOTALLY
RF

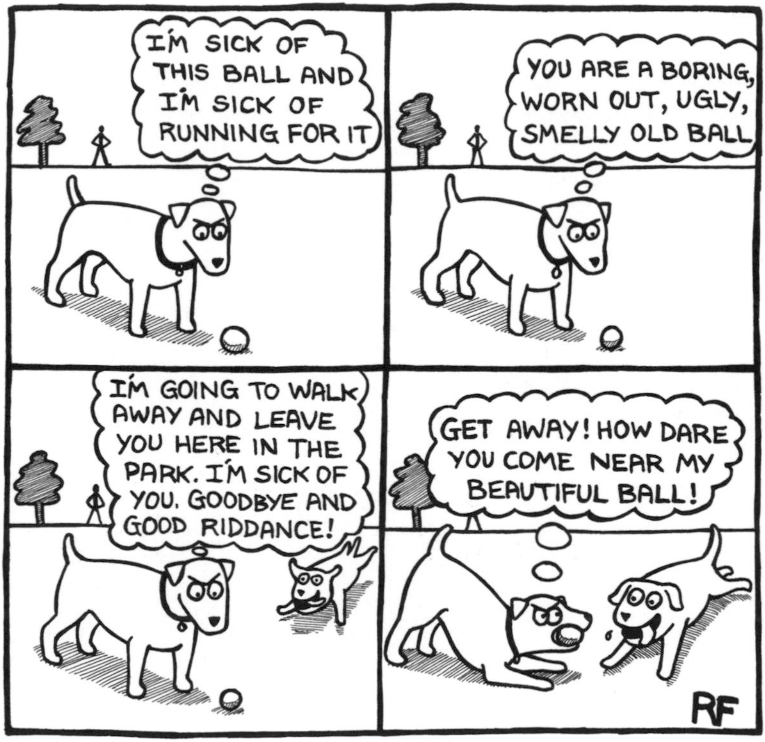
I'M SICK OF THIS BALL AND I'M SICK OF RUNNING FOR IT
YOU ARE A BORING, WORN OUT, UGLY, SMELLY OLD BALL
I'M GOING TO WALK AWAY AND LEAVE YOU HERE IN THE PARK. I'M SICK OF YOU. GOODBYE AND GOOD RIDDANCE!
GET AWAY! HOW DARE YOU COME NEAR MY BEAUTIFUL BALL!
RF

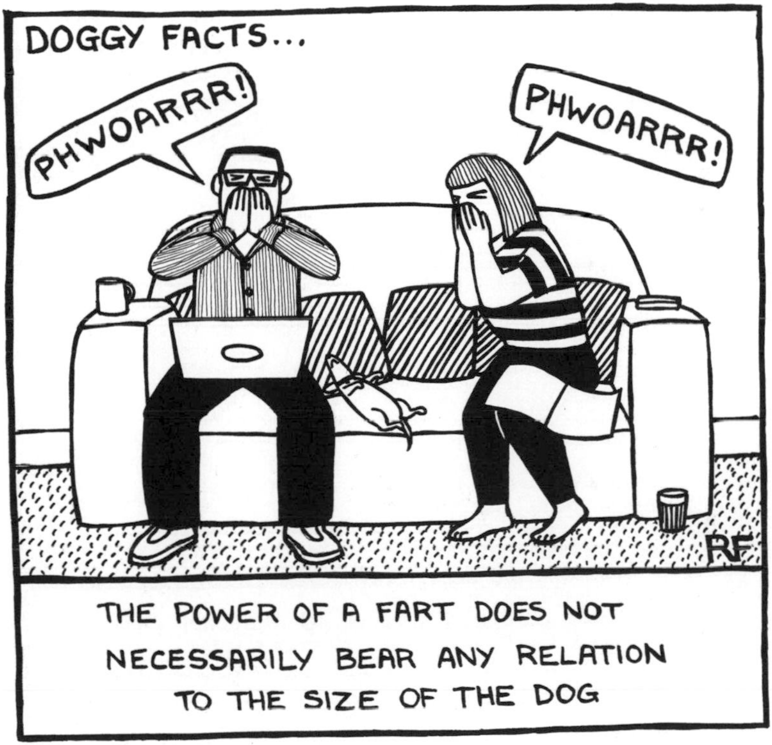
DOGGY FACTS...
PHWOARRR!
PHWOARRR!
RF
THE POWER OF A FART DOES NOT NECESSARILY BEAR ANY RELATION TO THE SIZE OF THE DOG

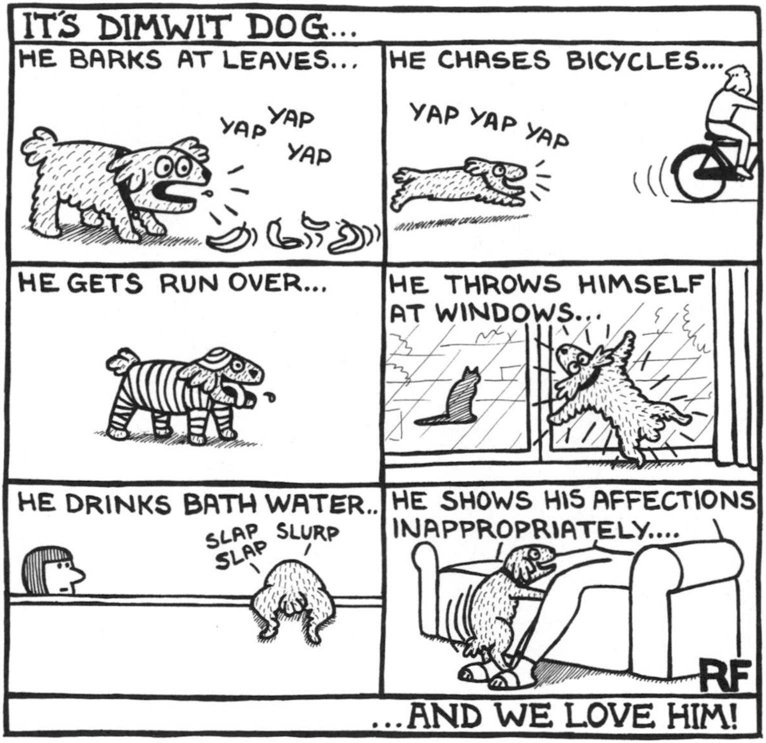
IT'S DIMWIT DOG...
HE BARKS AT LEAVES...
YAP YAP
YAP
HE CHASES BICYCLES...
YAP YAP YAP
HE GETS RUN OVER...
HE THROWS HIMSELF AT WINDOWS...
HE DRINKS BATH WATER..
SLAP SLAP
SLURP
HE SHOWS HIS AFFECTIONS INAPPROPRIATELY....
RF
...AND WE LOVE HIM!

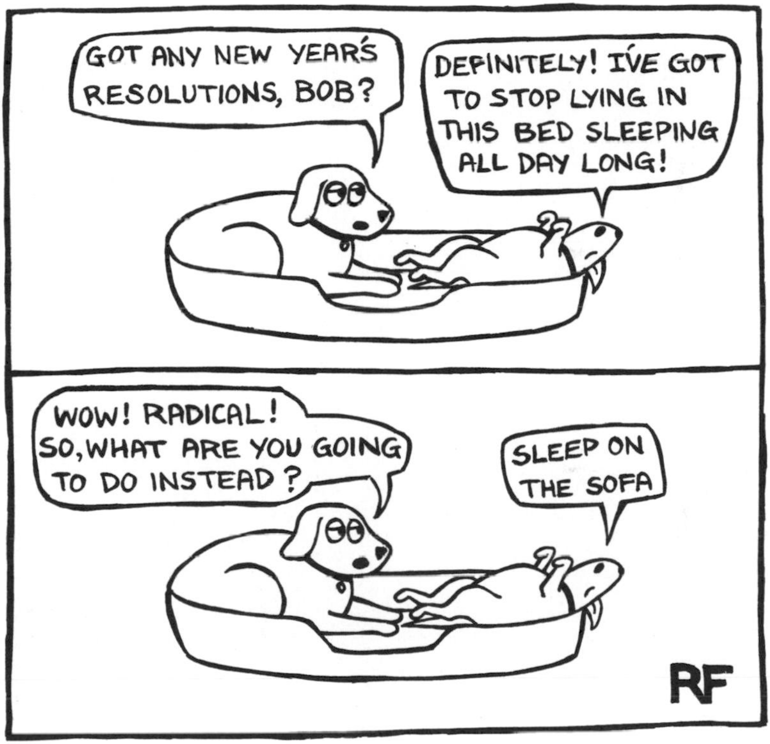
GOT ANY NEW YEAR'S RESOLUTIONS, BOB?
DEFINITELY! I'VE GOT TO STOP LYING IN THIS BED SLEEPING ALL DAY LONG!
WOW! RADICAL! SO, WHAT ARE YOU GOING TO DO INSTEAD?
SLEEP ON THE SOFA
RF

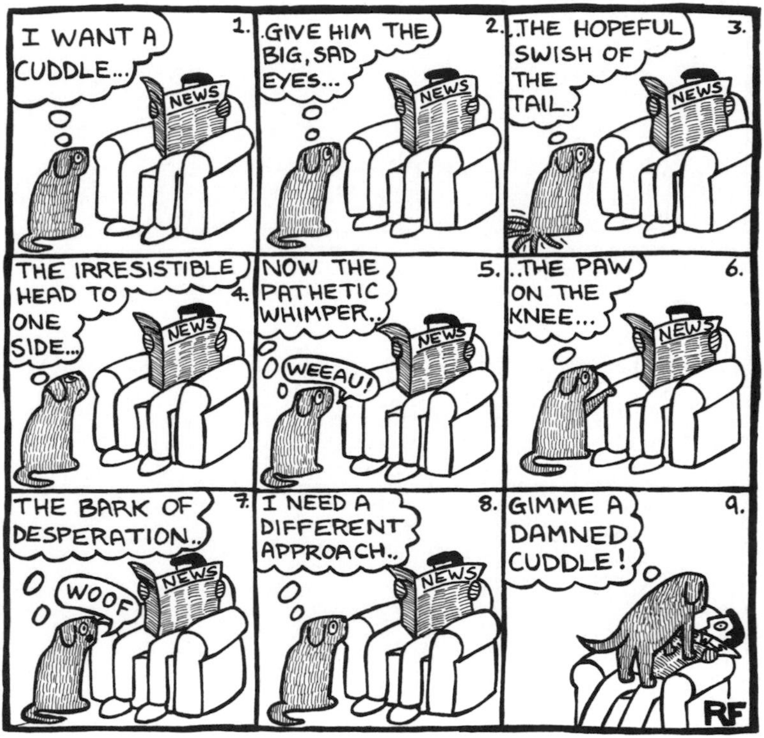

I WANT A CUDDLE...
1.
.GIVE HIM THE BIG, SAD EYES...
2.
.THE HOPEFUL SWISH OF THE TAIL..
3.
NEWS
THE IRRESISTIBLE HEAD TO ONE SIDE...
4.
NOW THE PATHETIC WHIMPER..
5.
WEEAU!
..THE PAW ON THE KNEE...
6.
THE BARK OF DESPERATION..
7.
WOOF
I NEED A DIFFERENT APPROACH..
8.
GIMME A DAMNED CUDDLE!
9.
RF

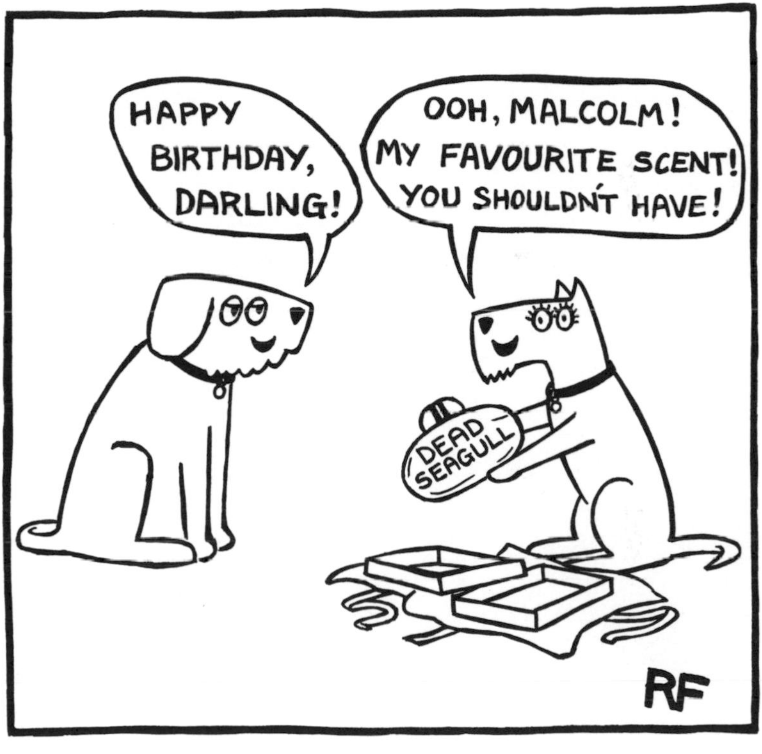
HAPPY BIRTHDAY, DARLING!
OOH, MALCOLM! MY FAVOURITE SCENT! YOU SHOULDN'T HAVE!
DEAD SEAGULL
RF

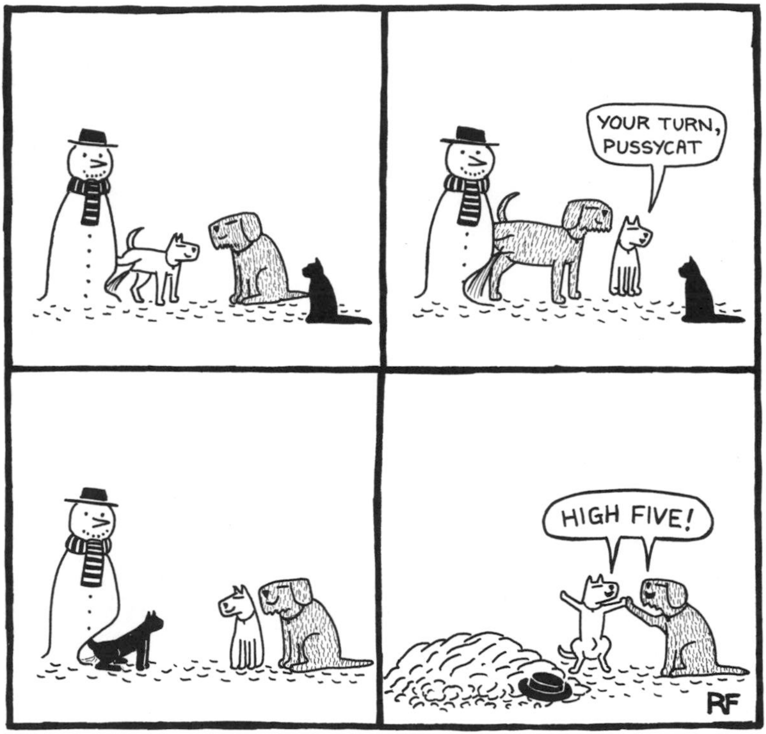
YOUR TURN, PUSSYCAT
HIGH FIVE!
RF

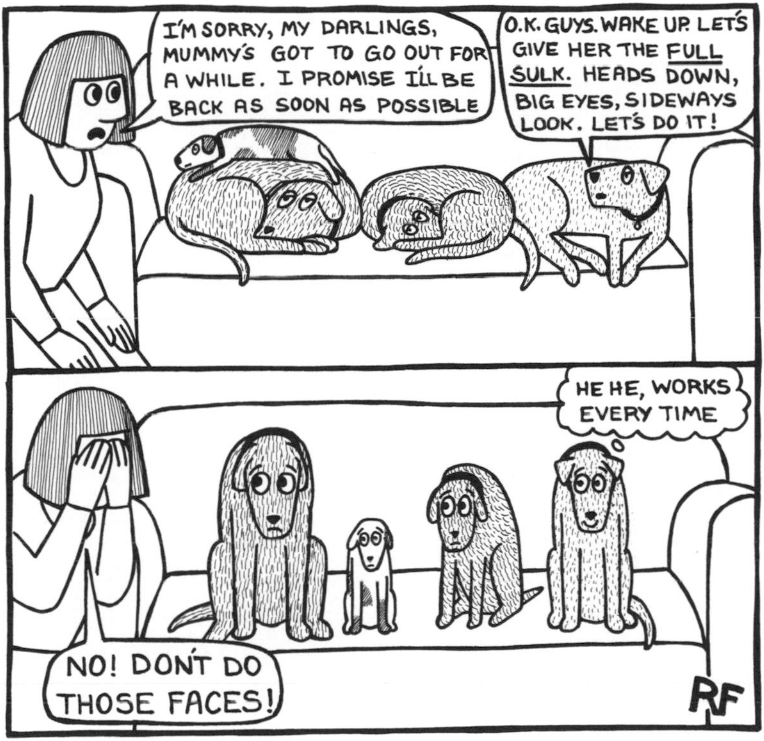
I'M SORRY, MY DARLINGS, MUMMY'S GOT TO GO OUT FOR A WHILE. I PROMISE I'LL BE BACK AS SOON AS POSSIBLE
O.K. GUYS. WAKE UP. LET'S GIVE HER THE FULL SULK. HEADS DOWN, BIG EYES, SIDEWAYS LOOK. LET'S DO IT!
HE HE, WORKS EVERY TIME
NO! DON'T DO THOSE FACES!
RF

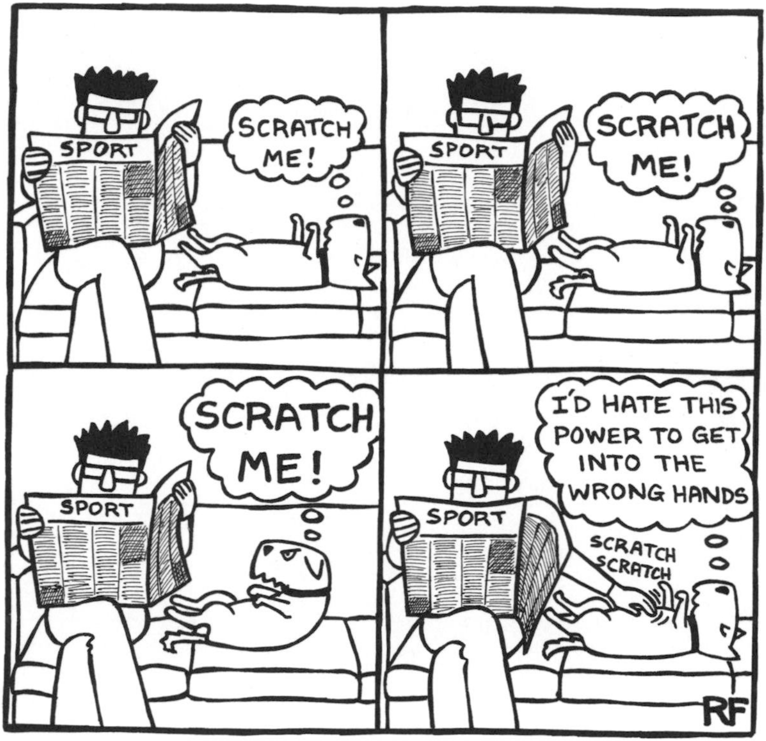
SPORT
SCRATCH ME!
SPORT
SCRATCH ME!
SPORT
SCRATCH ME!
SPORT
I'D HATE THIS POWER TO GET INTO THE WRONG HANDS
SCRATCH SCRATCH
RF

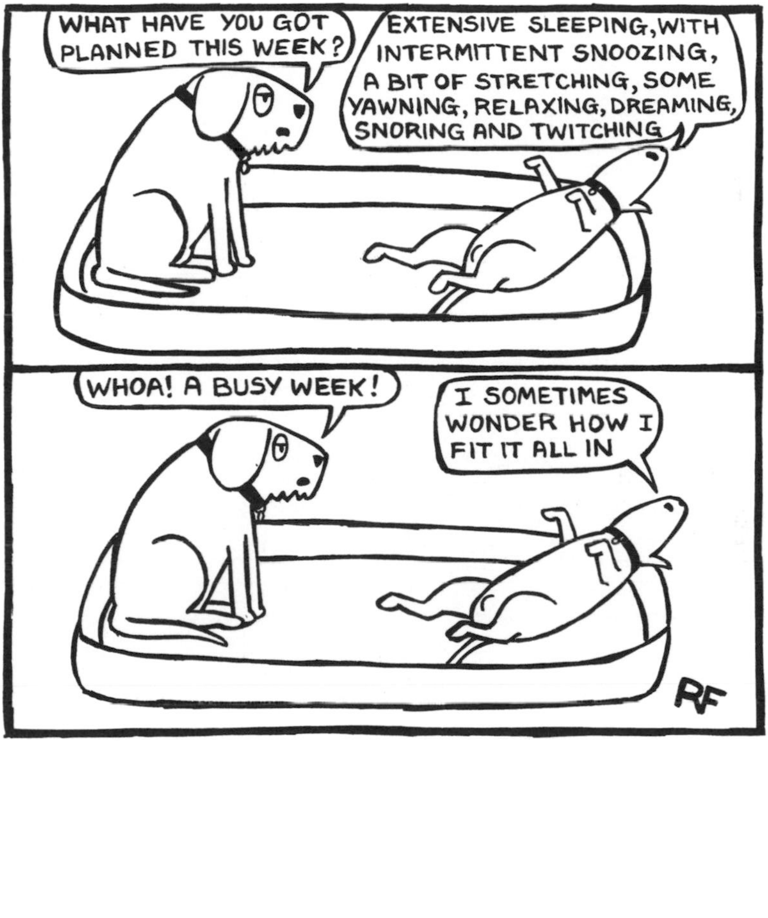
WHAT HAVE YOU GOT PLANNED THIS WEEK?
EXTENSIVE SLEEPING, WITH INTERMITTENT SNOOZING, A BIT OF STRETCHING, SOME YAWNING, RELAXING, DREAMING, SNORING AND TWITCHING
WHOA! A BUSY WEEK!
I SOMETIMES WONDER HOW I FIT IT ALL IN
RF

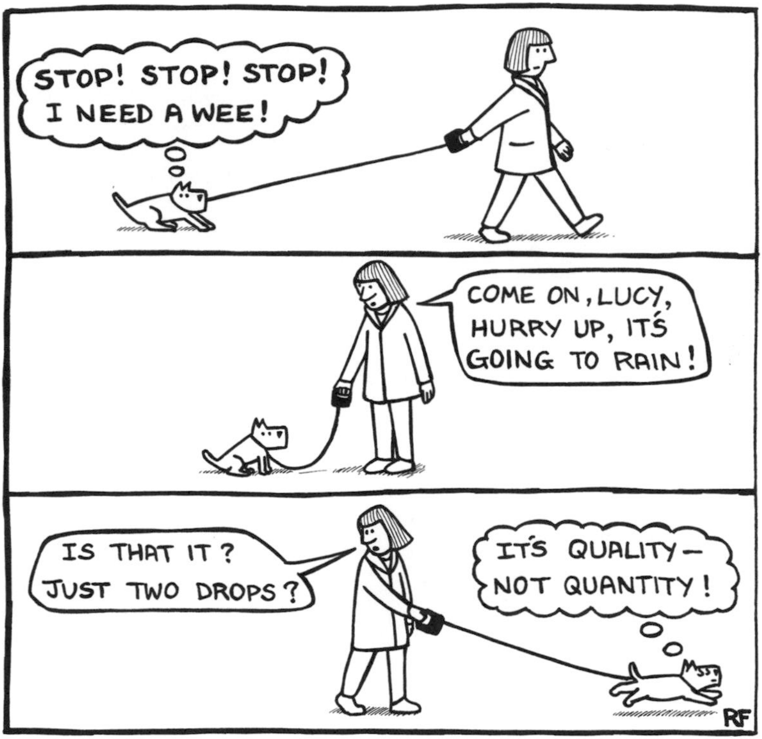
STOP! STOP! STOP! I NEED A WEE!
COME ON, LUCY, HURRY UP, IT'S GOING TO RAIN!
IS THAT IT? JUST TWO DROPS?
IT'S QUALITY – NOT QUANTITY!
RF

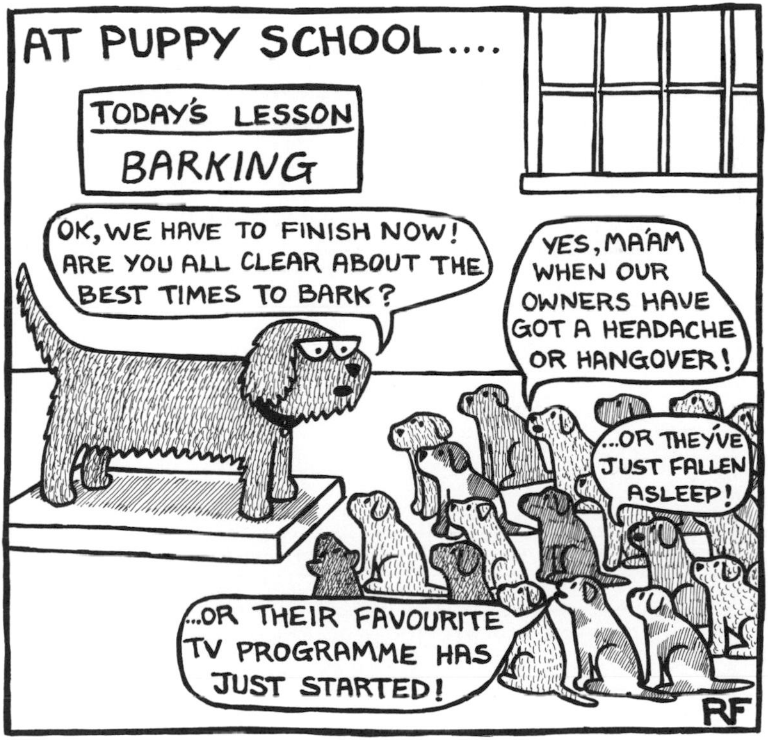
AT PUPPY SCHOOL....
TODAY'S LESSON
BARKING
OK, WE HAVE TO FINISH NOW! ARE YOU ALL CLEAR ABOUT THE BEST TIMES TO BARK?
YES, MA'AM WHEN OUR OWNERS HAVE GOT A HEADACHE OR HANGOVER!
...OR THEY'VE JUST FALLEN ASLEEP!
...OR THEIR FAVOURITE TV PROGRAMME HAS JUST STARTED!
RF

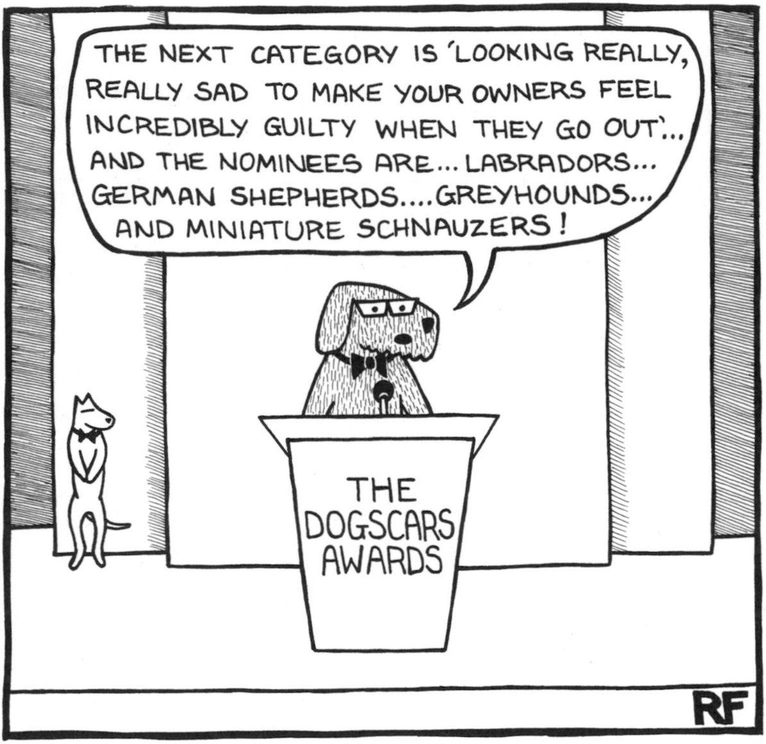
THE NEXT CATEGORY IS 'LOOKING REALLY, REALLY SAD TO MAKE YOUR OWNERS FEEL INCREDIBLY GUILTY WHEN THEY GO OUT'... AND THE NOMINEES ARE... LABRADORS... GERMAN SHEPHERDS....GREYHOUNDS... AND MINIATURE SCHNAUZERS!
THE DOGSCARS AWARDS
RF

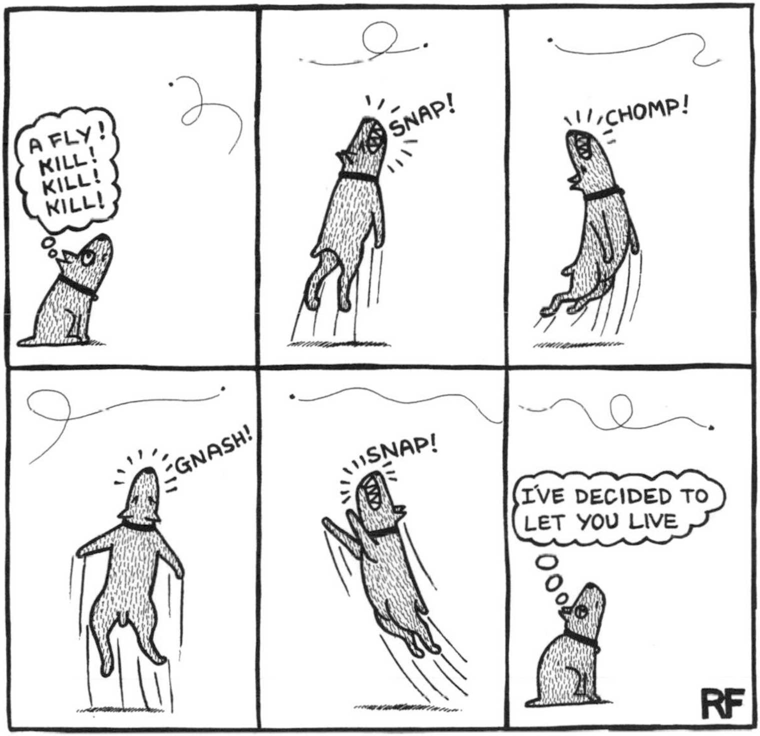
A FLY! KILL! KILL! KILL!
SNAP!
CHOMP!
GNASH!
SNAP!
I'VE DECIDED TO LET YOU LIVE
RF

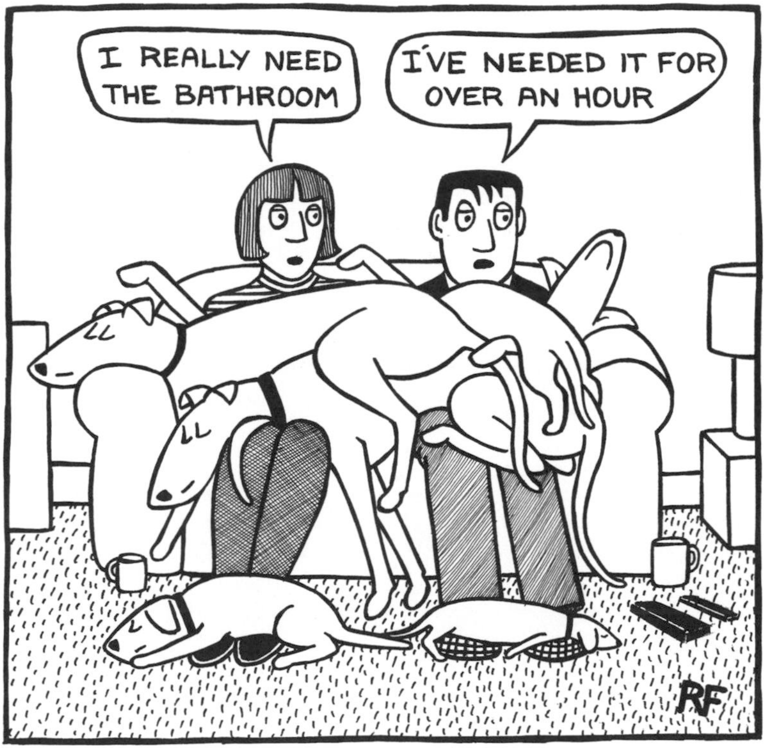
I REALLY NEED THE BATHROOM
I'VE NEEDED IT FOR OVER AN HOUR
RF

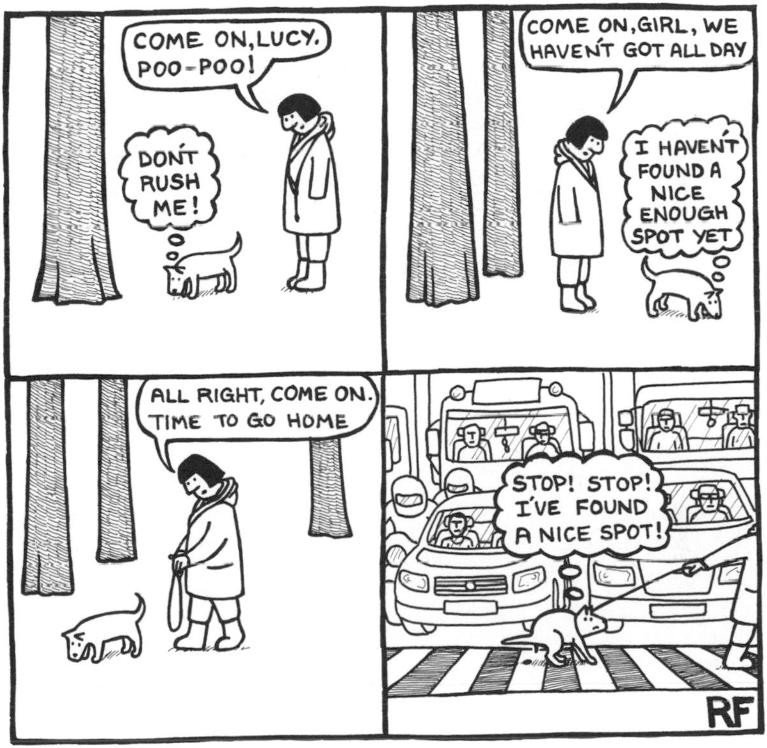
COME ON, LUCY. POO-POO!
DON'T RUSH ME!
COME ON, GIRL, WE HAVEN'T GOT ALL DAY
I HAVEN'T FOUND A NICE ENOUGH SPOT YET
ALL RIGHT, COME ON. TIME TO GO HOME
STOP! STOP! I'VE FOUND A NICE SPOT!
RF

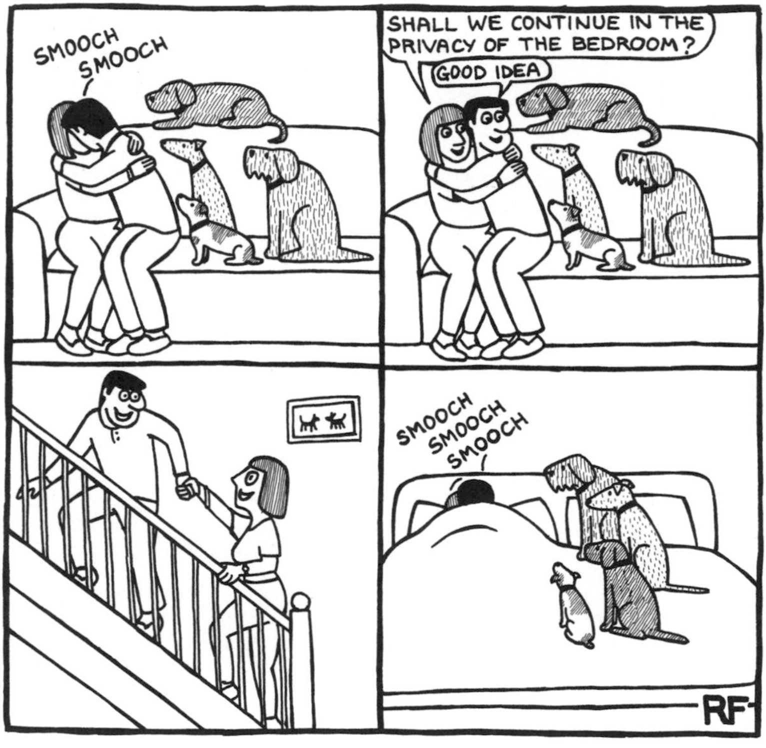
SMOOCH
SMOOCH
SHALL WE CONTINUE IN THE PRIVACY OF THE BEDROOM?
GOOD IDEA
SMOOCH
SMOOCH
SMOOCH
RF

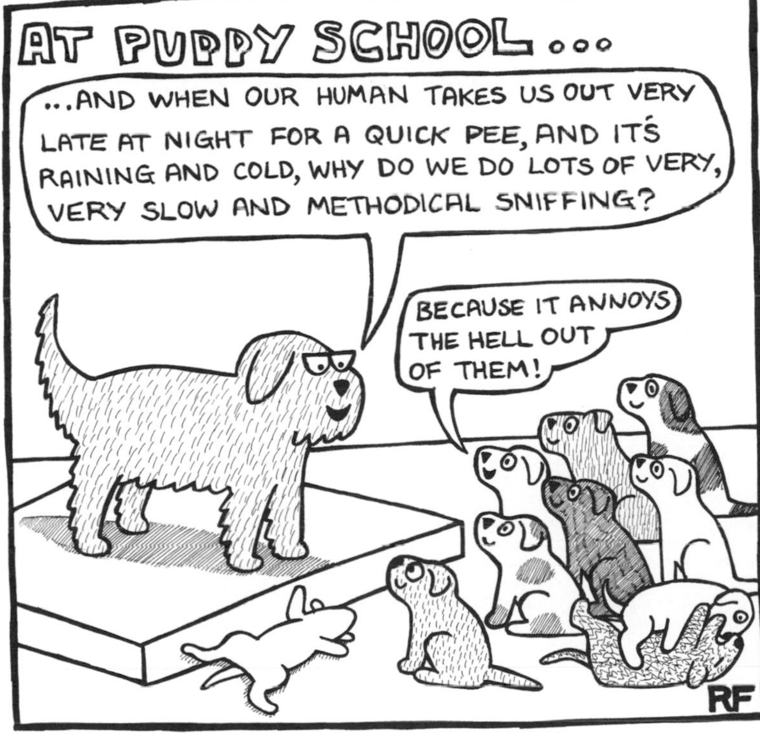
AT PUPPY SCHOOL...
...AND WHEN OUR HUMAN TAKES US OUT VERY LATE AT NIGHT FOR A QUICK PEE, AND IT'S RAINING AND COLD, WHY DO WE DO LOTS OF VERY, VERY SLOW AND METHODICAL SNIFFING?
BECAUSE IT ANNOYS THE HELL OUT OF THEM!
RF

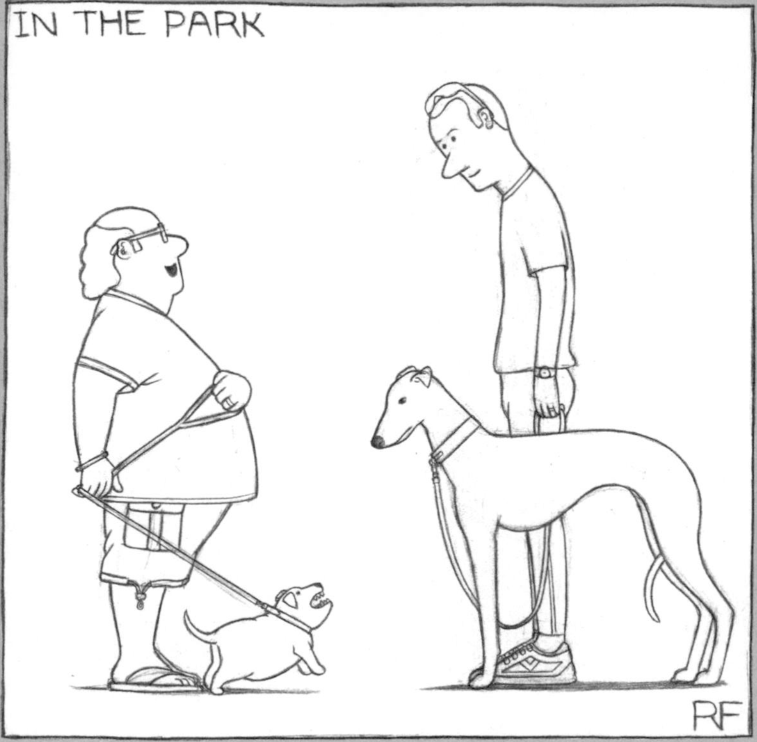
IN THE PARK
RF

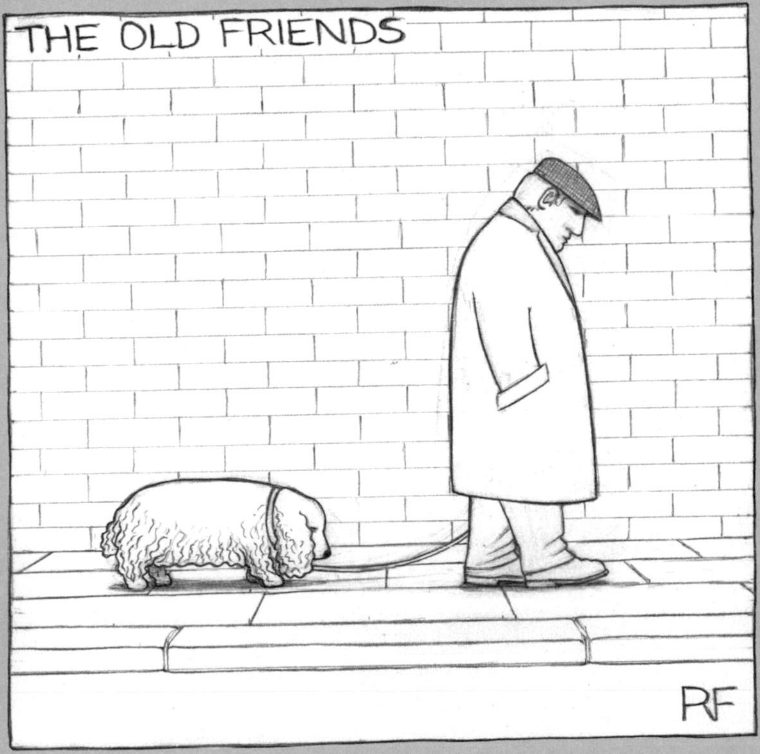
THE OLD FRIENDS
RF

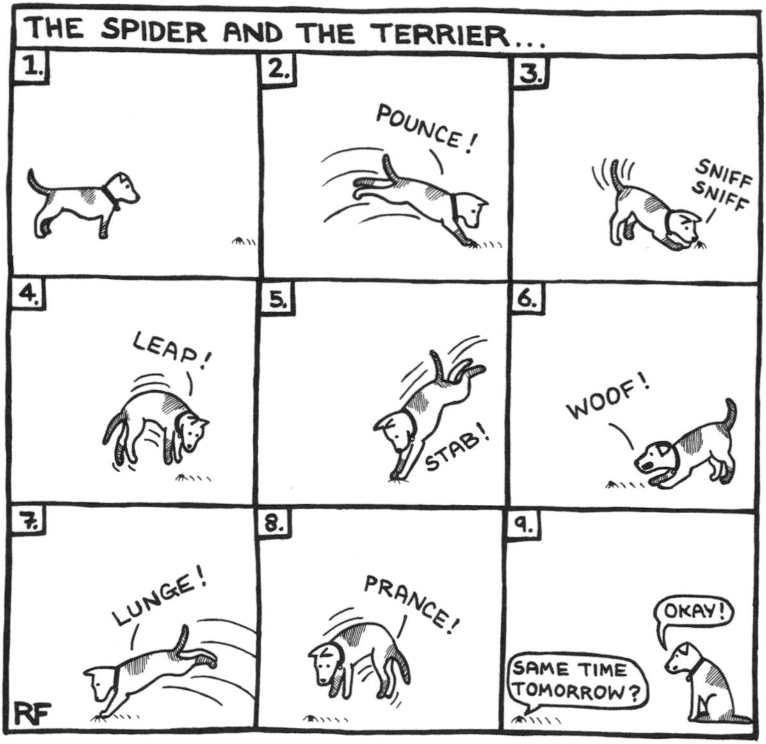
THE SPIDER AND THE TERRIER...
1.
2.
POUNCE!
3.
SNIFF SNIFF
4.
LEAP!
5.
STAB!
6.
WOOF!
7.
LUNGE!
RF
8.
PRANCE!
9.
SAME TIME TOMORROW?
OKAY!

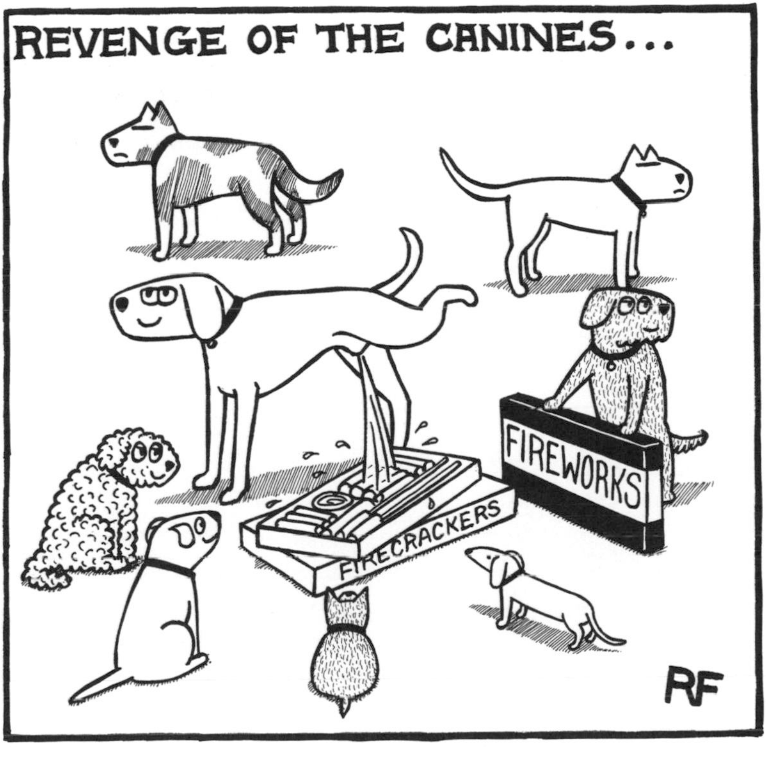
REVENGE OF THE CANINES...
FIREWORKS
FIRECRACKERS
RF

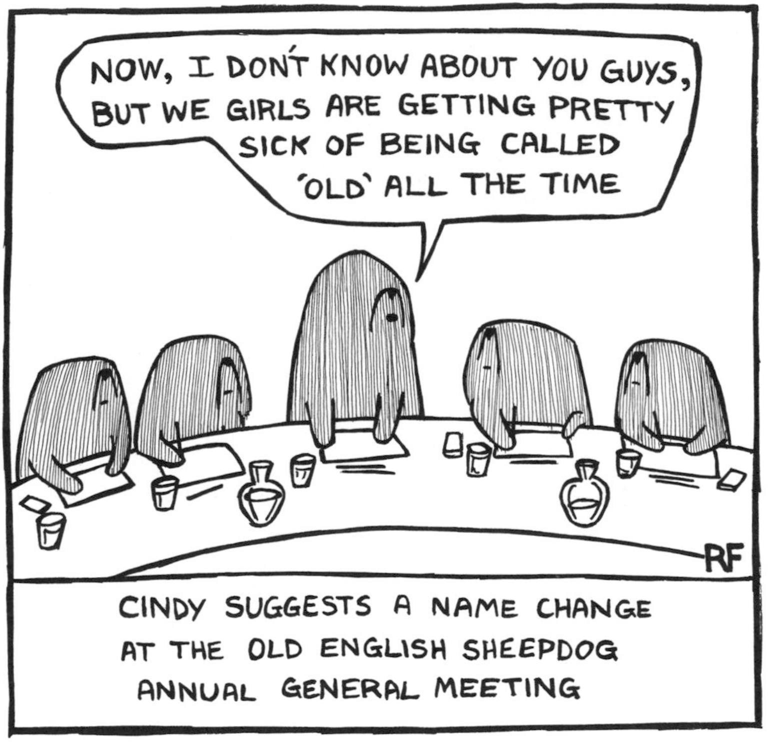
NOW, I DON'T KNOW ABOUT YOU GUYS, BUT WE GIRLS ARE GETTING PRETTY SICK OF BEING CALLED 'OLD' ALL THE TIME
RF

CINDY SUGGESTS A NAME CHANGE AT THE OLD ENGLISH SHEEPDOG ANNUAL GENERAL MEETING

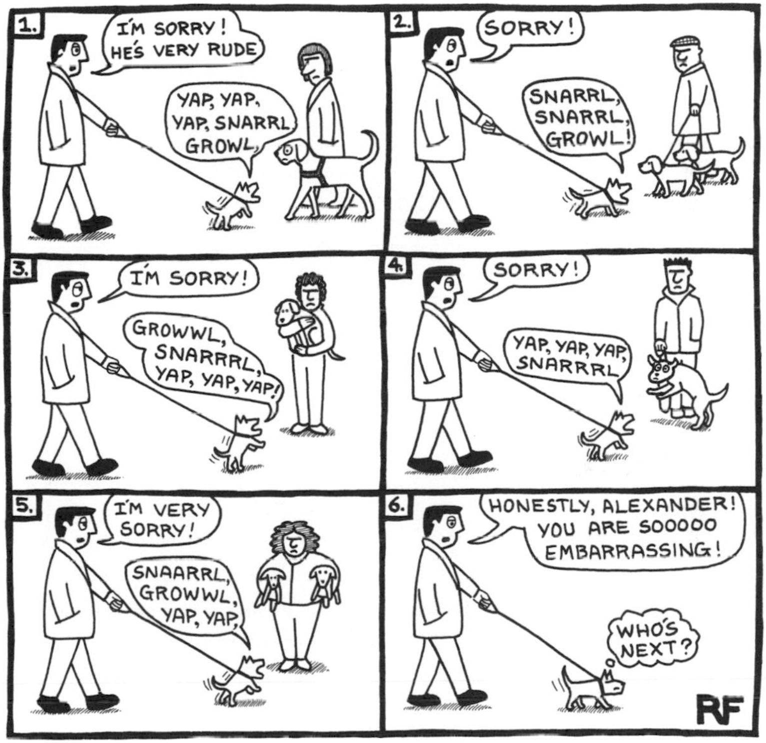
1.
I'M SORRY! HE'S VERY RUDE
YAP, YAP, YAP, SNARRL GROWL,
2.
SORRY!
SNARRL, SNARRL, GROWL!
3.
I'M SORRY!
GROWWL, SNARRRL, YAP, YAP, YAP!
4.
SORRY!
YAP, YAP, YAP, SNARRRL
5.
I'M VERY SORRY!
SNAARRL, GROWWL, YAP, YAP,
6.
HONESTLY, ALEXANDER! YOU ARE SOOOOO EMBARRASSING!
WHO'S NEXT?
RF

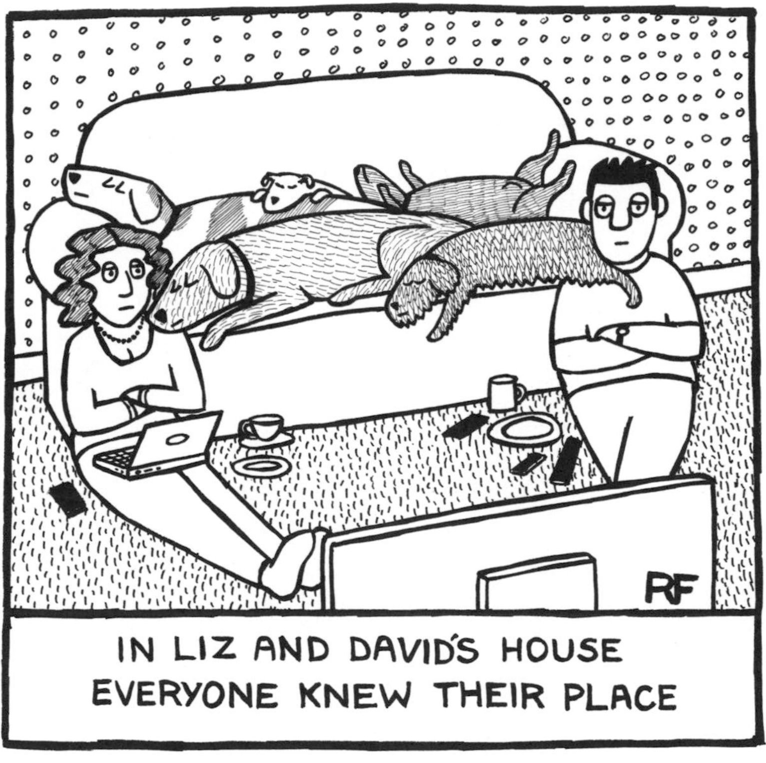
RF

IN LIZ AND DAVID'S HOUSE
EVERYONE KNEW THEIR PLACE

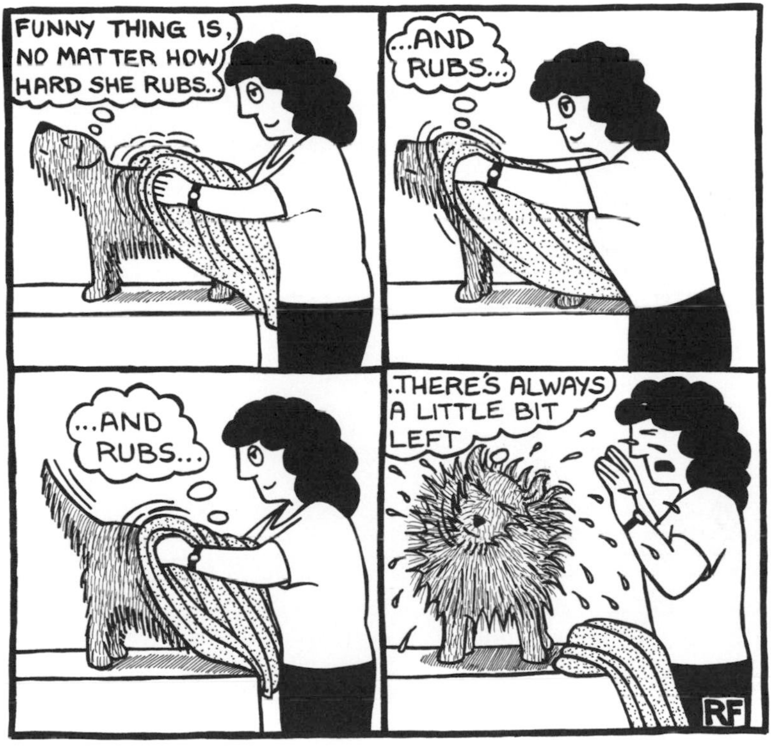
FUNNY THING IS, NO MATTER HOW HARD SHE RUBS...
...AND RUBS...
...AND RUBS...
..THERE'S ALWAYS A LITTLE BIT LEFT
RF

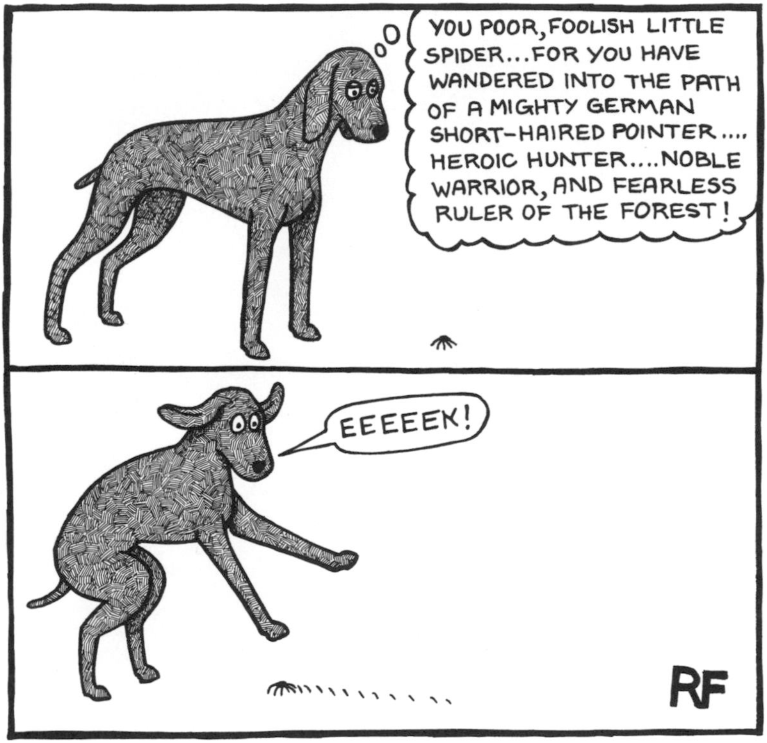
YOU POOR, FOOLISH LITTLE SPIDER... FOR YOU HAVE WANDERED INTO THE PATH OF A MIGHTY GERMAN SHORT-HAIRED POINTER.... HEROIC HUNTER.... NOBLE WARRIOR, AND FEARLESS RULER OF THE FOREST!
EEEEEK!
RF

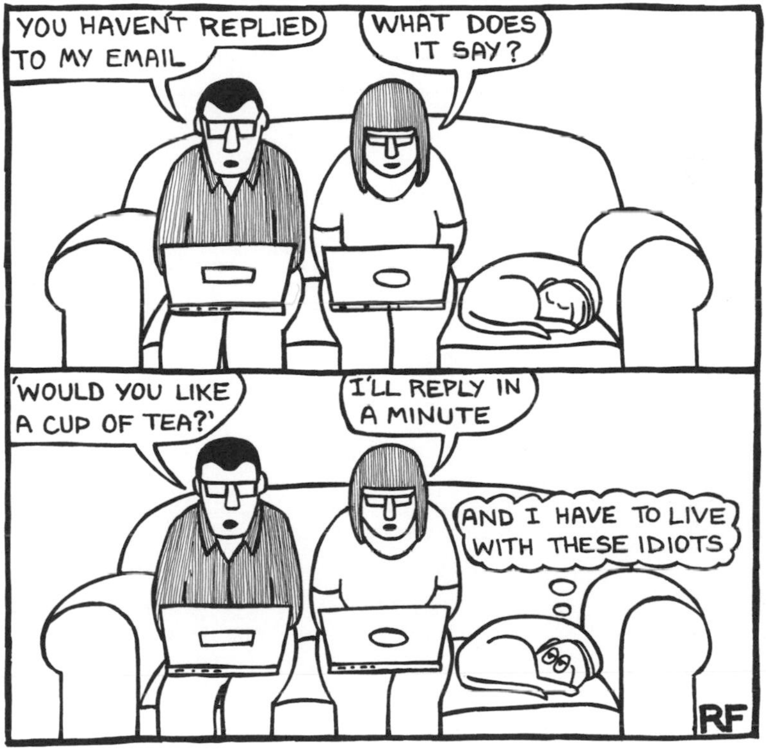
YOU HAVEN'T REPLIED TO MY EMAIL
WHAT DOES IT SAY?
'WOULD YOU LIKE A CUP OF TEA?'
I'LL REPLY IN A MINUTE
AND I HAVE TO LIVE WITH THESE IDIOTS
RF

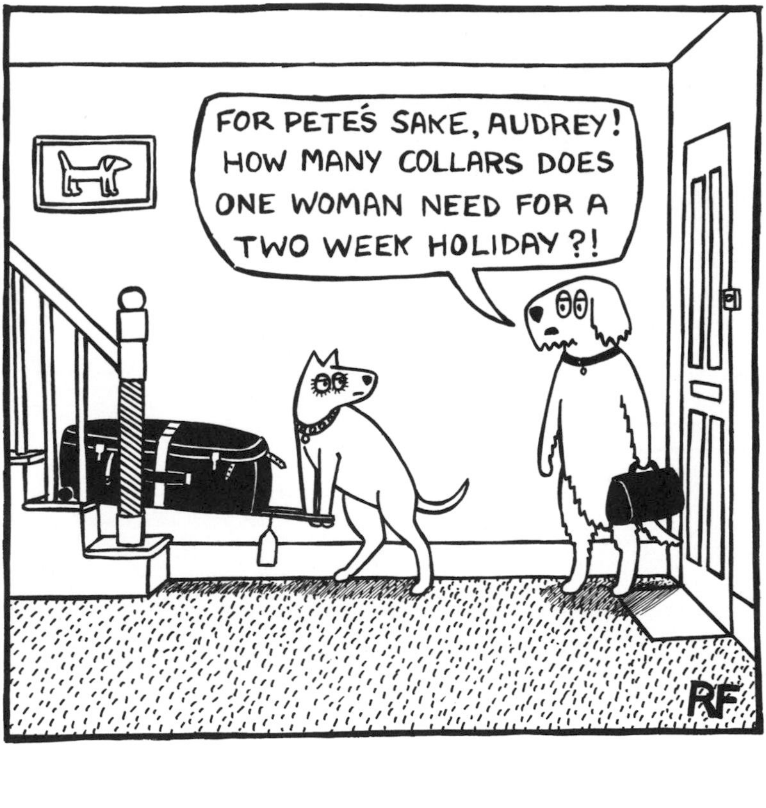
FOR PETE'S SAKE, AUDREY! HOW MANY COLLARS DOES ONE WOMAN NEED FOR A TWO WEEK HOLIDAY?!
RF

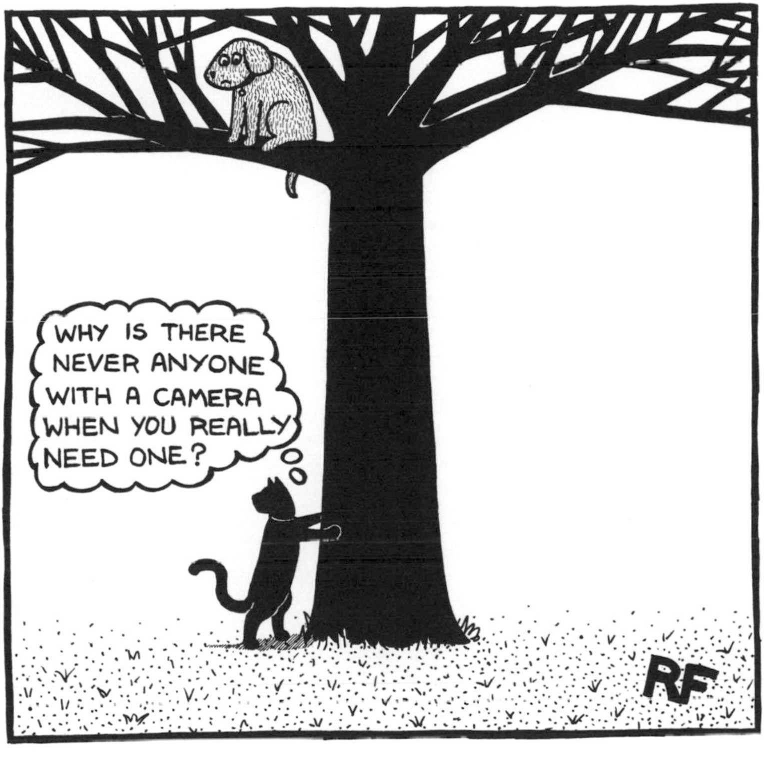
WHY IS THERE NEVER ANYONE WITH A CAMERA WHEN YOU REALLY NEED ONE?
RF

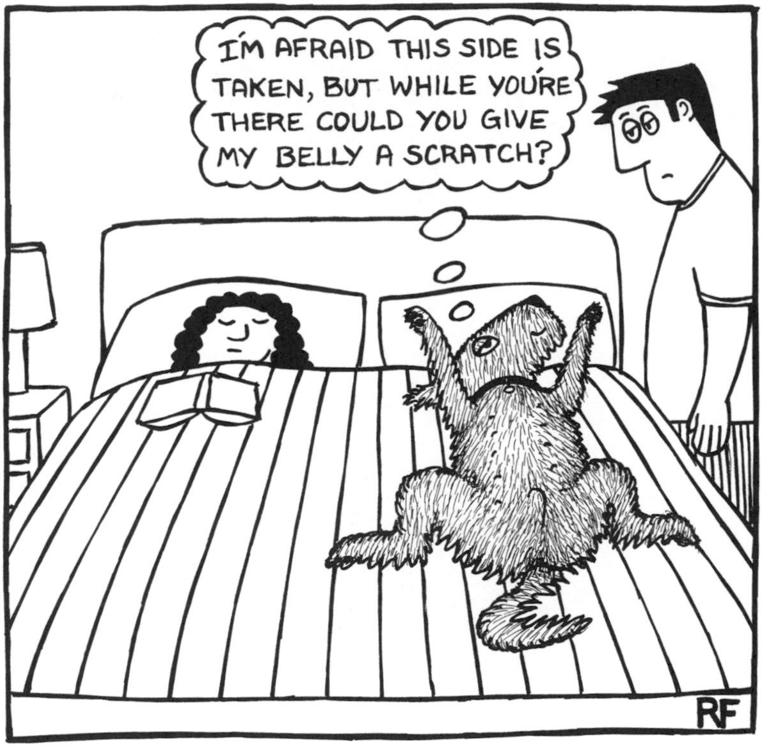
I'M AFRAID THIS SIDE IS TAKEN, BUT WHILE YOU'RE THERE COULD YOU GIVE MY BELLY A SCRATCH?
RF

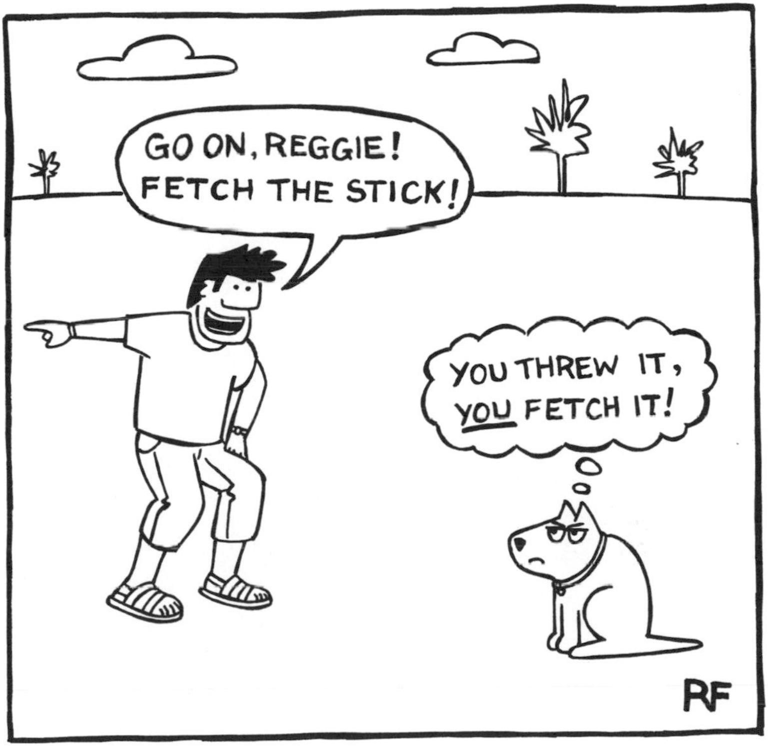
GO ON, REGGIE! FETCH THE STICK!
YOU THREW IT, YOU FETCH IT!
RF

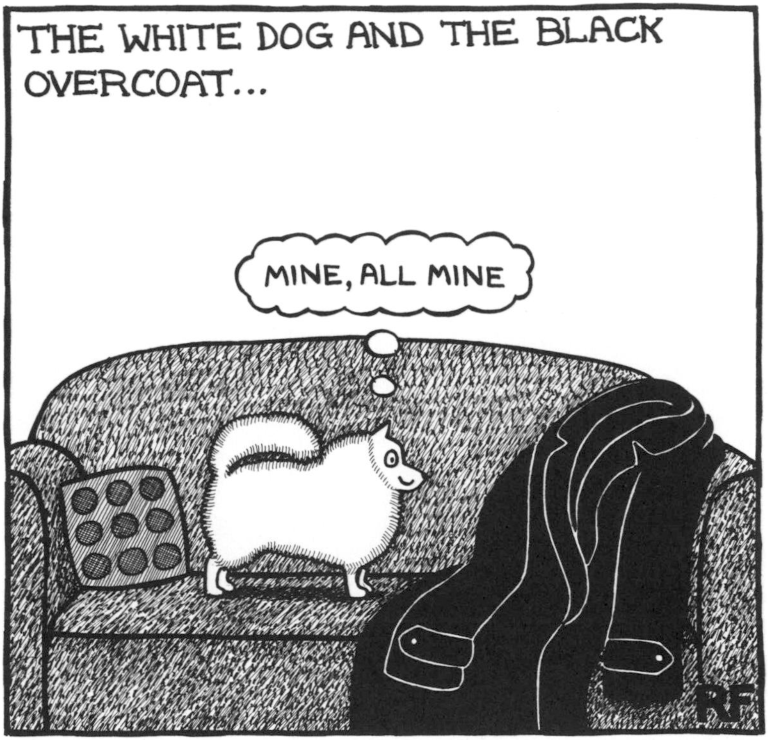
THE WHITE DOG AND THE BLACK OVERCOAT...
MINE, ALL MINE
RF

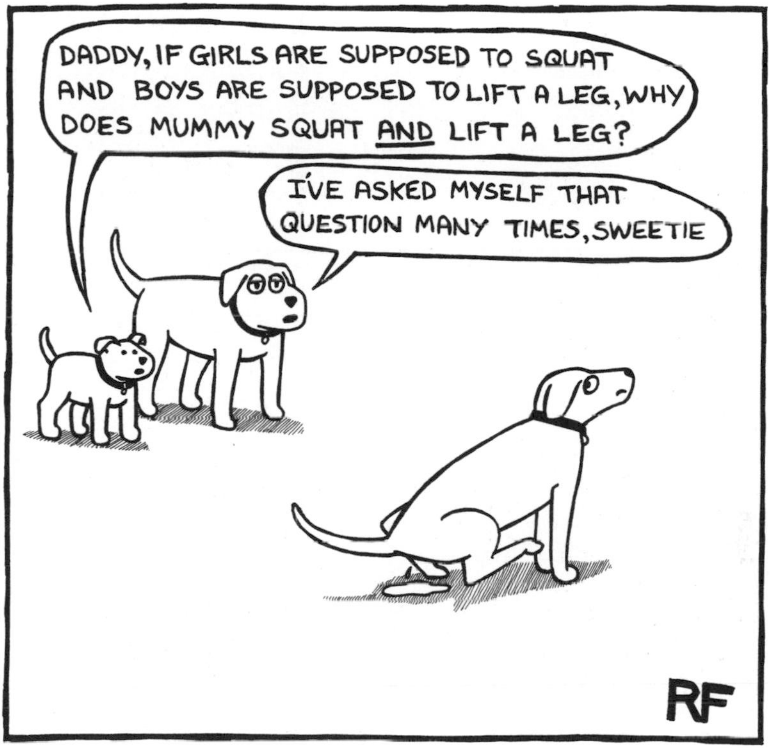
DADDY, IF GIRLS ARE SUPPOSED TO SQUAT AND BOYS ARE SUPPOSED TO LIFT A LEG, WHY DOES MUMMY SQUAT AND LIFT A LEG?
I'VE ASKED MYSELF THAT QUESTION MANY TIMES, SWEETIE
RF

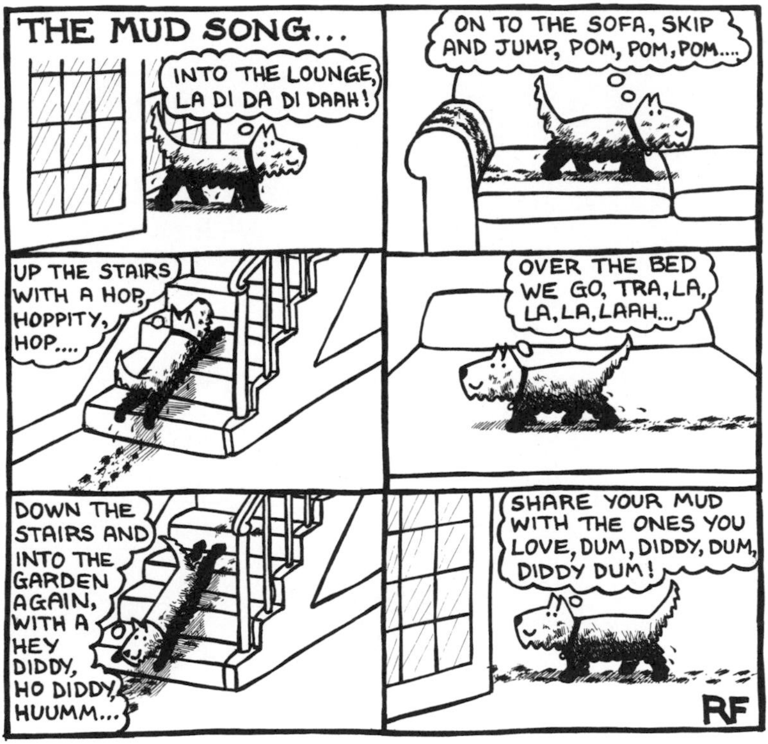
THE MUD SONG...
INTO THE LOUNGE, LA DI DA DI DAAH!
ON TO THE SOFA, SKIP AND JUMP, POM, POM, POM....
UP THE STAIRS WITH A HOP, HOPPITY, HOP....
OVER THE BED WE GO, TRA, LA, LA, LA, LAAH...
DOWN THE STAIRS AND INTO THE GARDEN AGAIN, WITH A HEY DIDDY, HO DIDDY, HUUMM...
SHARE YOUR MUD WITH THE ONES YOU LOVE, DUM, DIDDY, DUM, DIDDY DUM!
RF

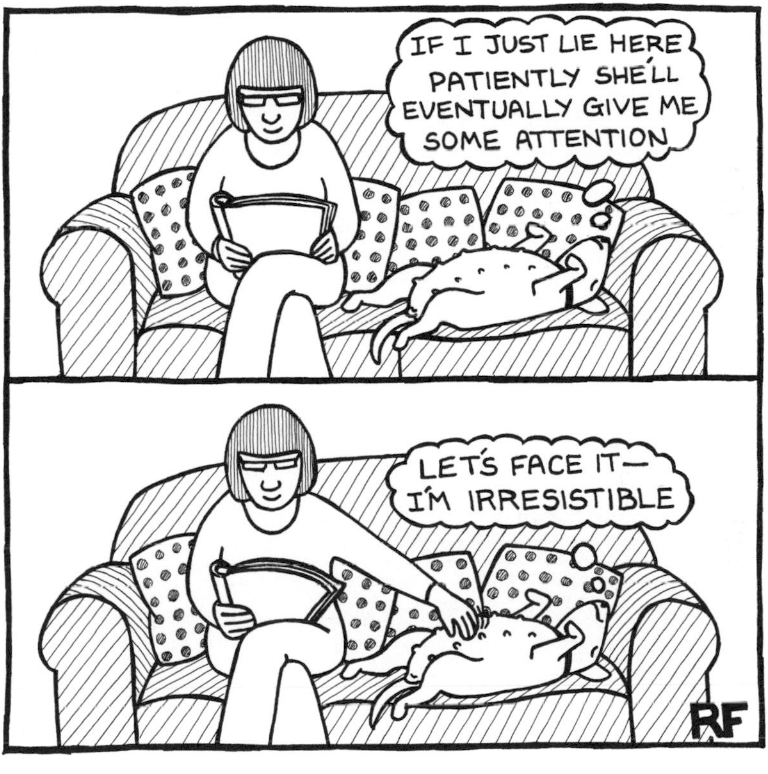

IF I JUST LIE HERE PATIENTLY SHE'LL EVENTUALLY GIVE ME SOME ATTENTION
LET'S FACE IT— I'M IRRESISTIBLE
RF

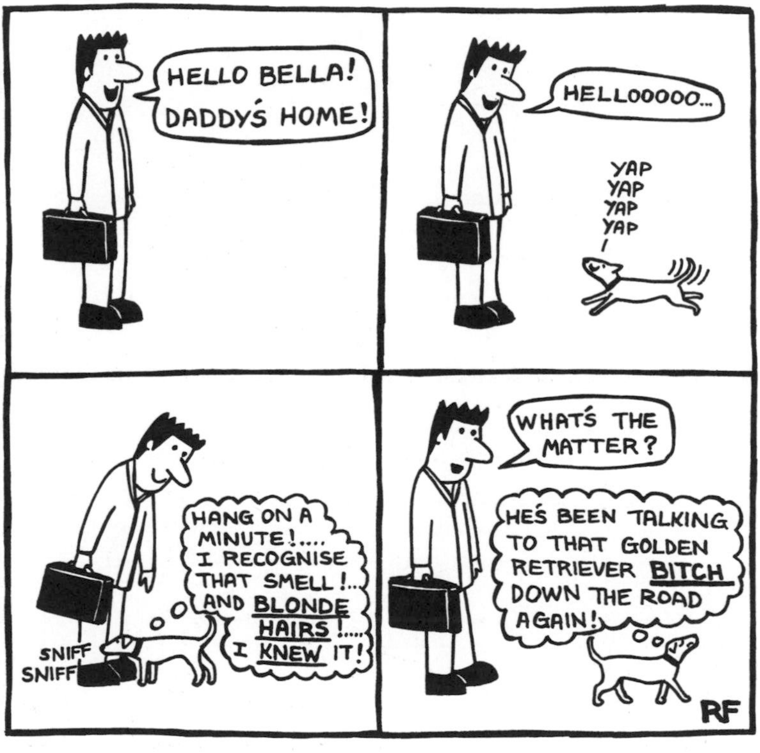
HELLO BELLA! DADDY'S HOME!
HELLOOOOO...
YAP YAP YAP YAP
SNIFF SNIFF
HANG ON A MINUTE!.... I RECOGNISE THAT SMELL!.. AND BLONDE HAIRS!.... I KNEW IT!
WHAT'S THE MATTER?
HE'S BEEN TALKING TO THAT GOLDEN RETRIEVER BITCH DOWN THE ROAD AGAIN!
RF

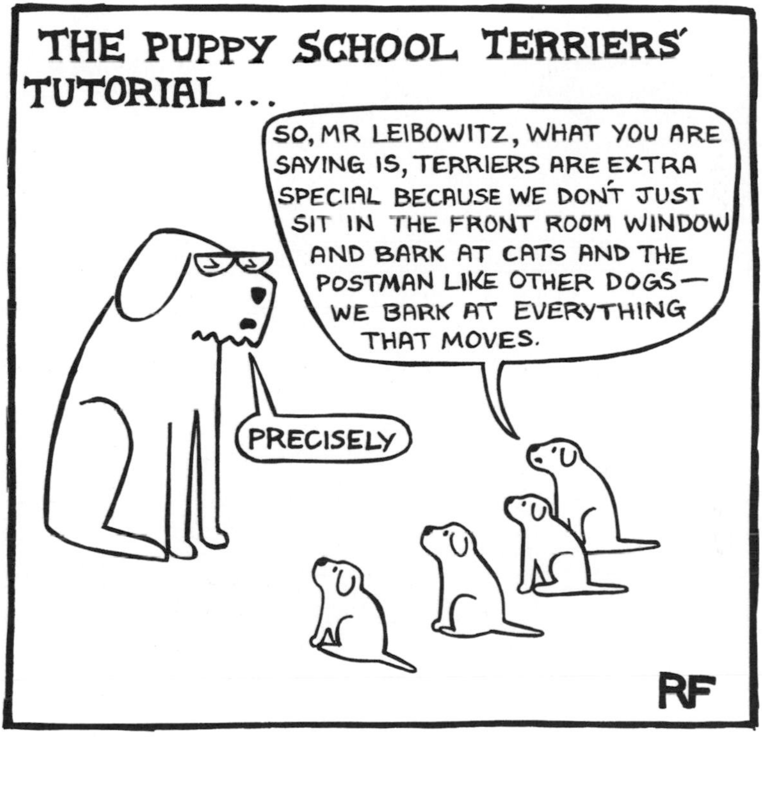
THE PUPPY SCHOOL TERRIERS' TUTORIAL...
SO, MR LEIBOWITZ, WHAT YOU ARE SAYING IS, TERRIERS ARE EXTRA SPECIAL BECAUSE WE DON'T JUST SIT IN THE FRONT ROOM WINDOW AND BARK AT CATS AND THE POSTMAN LIKE OTHER DOGS— WE BARK AT EVERYTHING THAT MOVES.
PRECISELY
RF

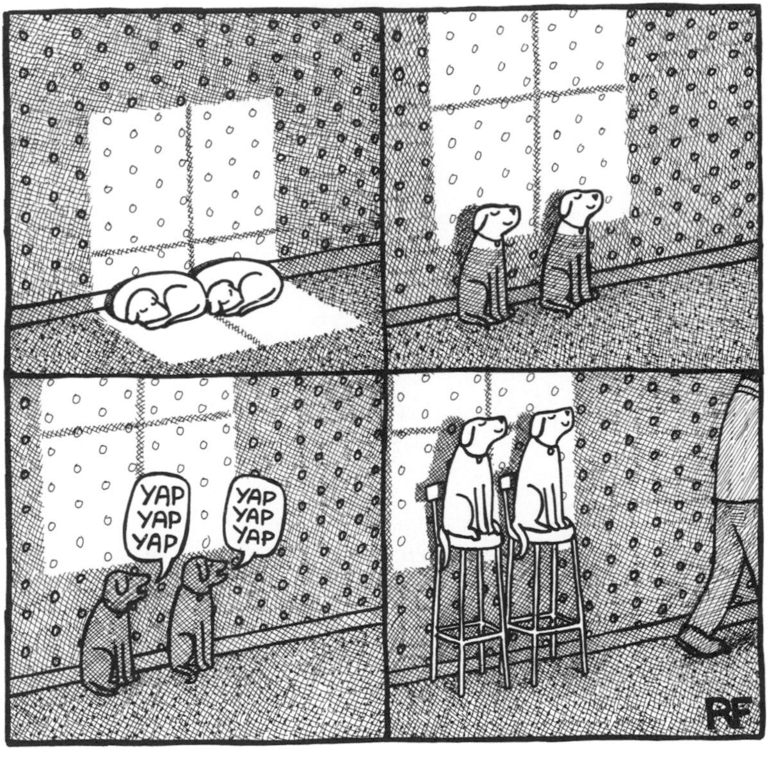
YAP
YAP
YAP
YAP
YAP
YAP
RF

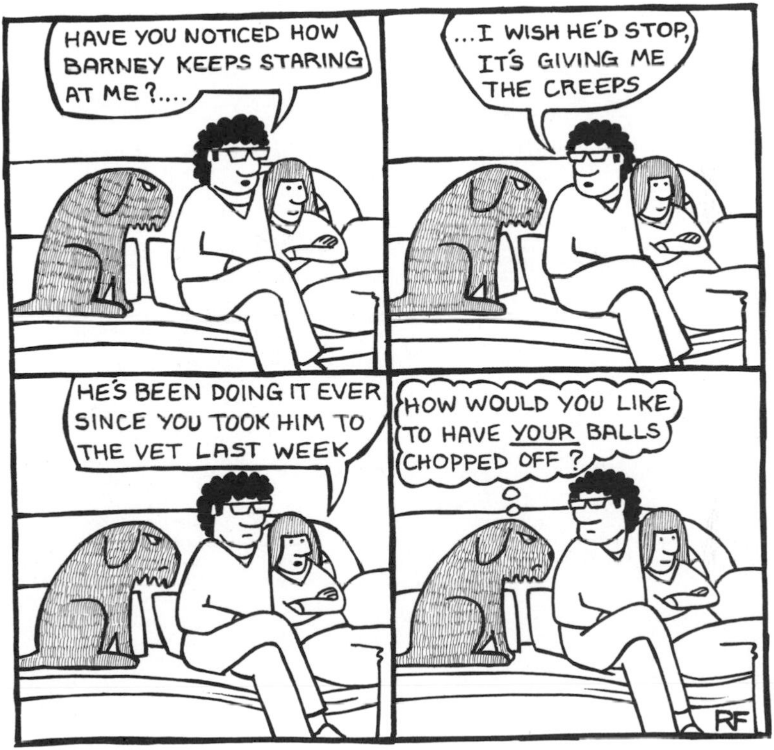
HAVE YOU NOTICED HOW BARNEY KEEPS STARING AT ME ?....
...I WISH HE'D STOP, IT'S GIVING ME THE CREEPS
HE'S BEEN DOING IT EVER SINCE YOU TOOK HIM TO THE VET LAST WEEK
HOW WOULD YOU LIKE TO HAVE YOUR BALLS CHOPPED OFF ?
RF

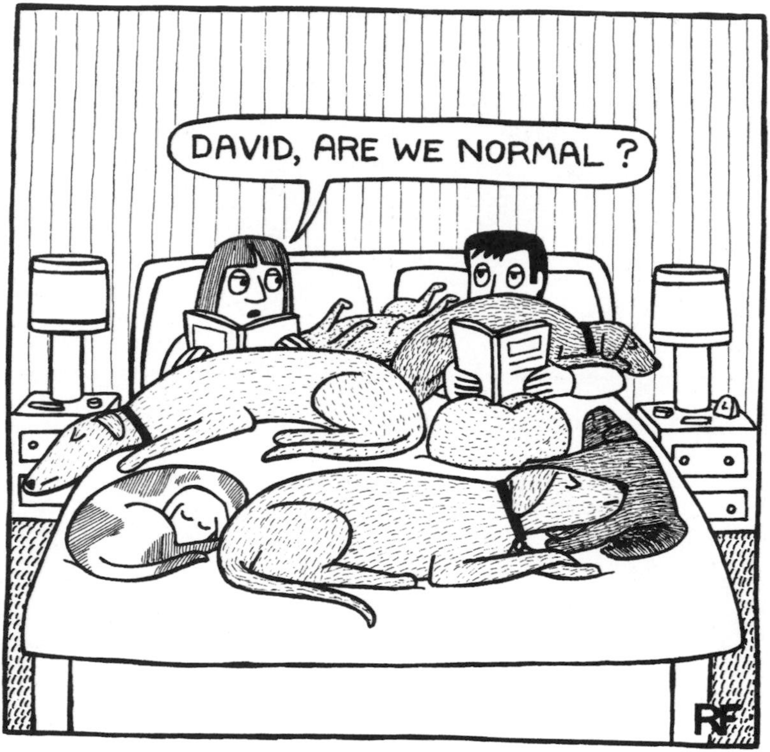
DAVID, ARE WE NORMAL ?
RF

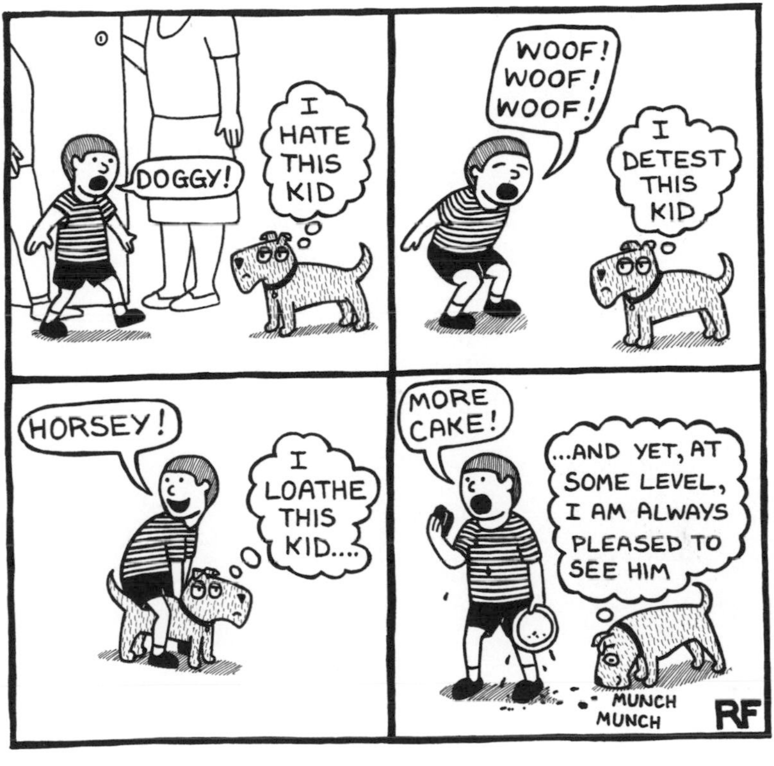
DOGGY!
I HATE THIS KID
WOOF! WOOF! WOOF!
I DETEST THIS KID
HORSEY!
I LOATHE THIS KID....
MORE CAKE!
...AND YET, AT SOME LEVEL, I AM ALWAYS PLEASED TO SEE HIM
MUNCH MUNCH
RF

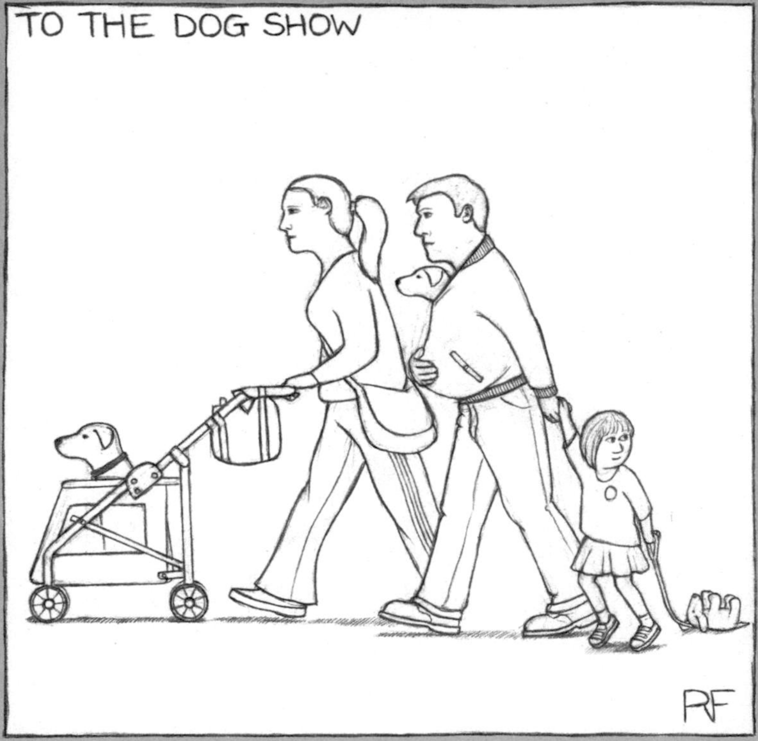
TO THE DOG SHOW
RF

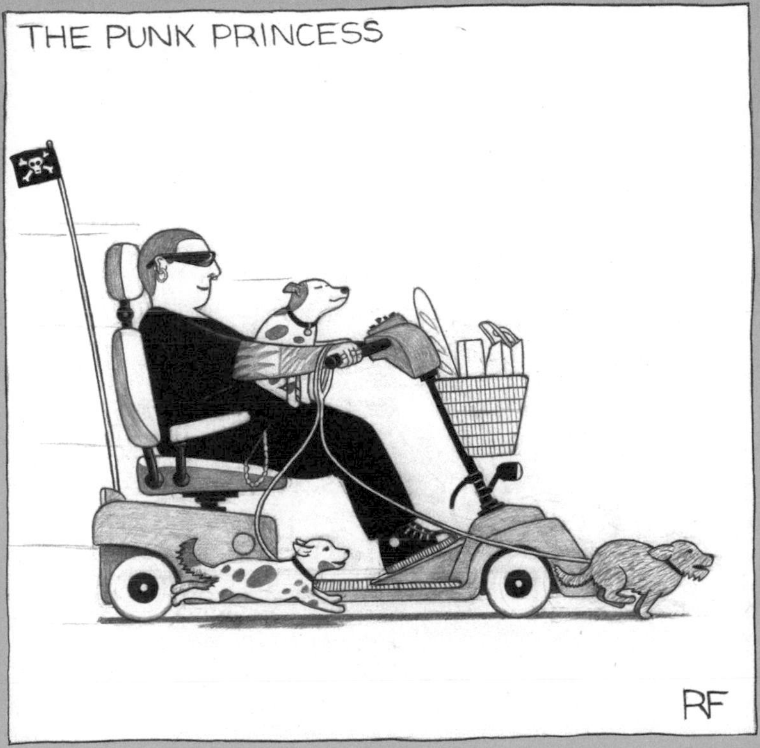
THE PUNK PRINCESS
RF

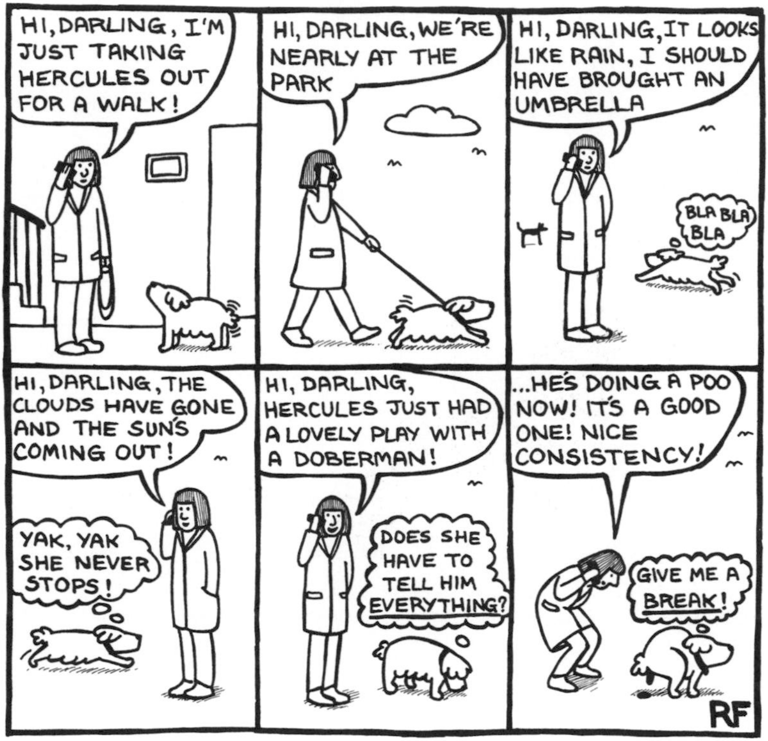
HI, DARLING, I'M JUST TAKING HERCULES OUT FOR A WALK!
HI, DARLING, WE'RE NEARLY AT THE PARK
HI, DARLING, IT LOOKS LIKE RAIN, I SHOULD HAVE BROUGHT AN UMBRELLA
BLA BLA BLA
HI, DARLING, THE CLOUDS HAVE GONE AND THE SUN'S COMING OUT!
YAK, YAK SHE NEVER STOPS!
HI, DARLING, HERCULES JUST HAD A LOVELY PLAY WITH A DOBERMAN!
DOES SHE HAVE TO TELL HIM EVERYTHING?
...HE'S DOING A POO NOW! IT'S A GOOD ONE! NICE CONSISTENCY!
GIVE ME A BREAK!
RF

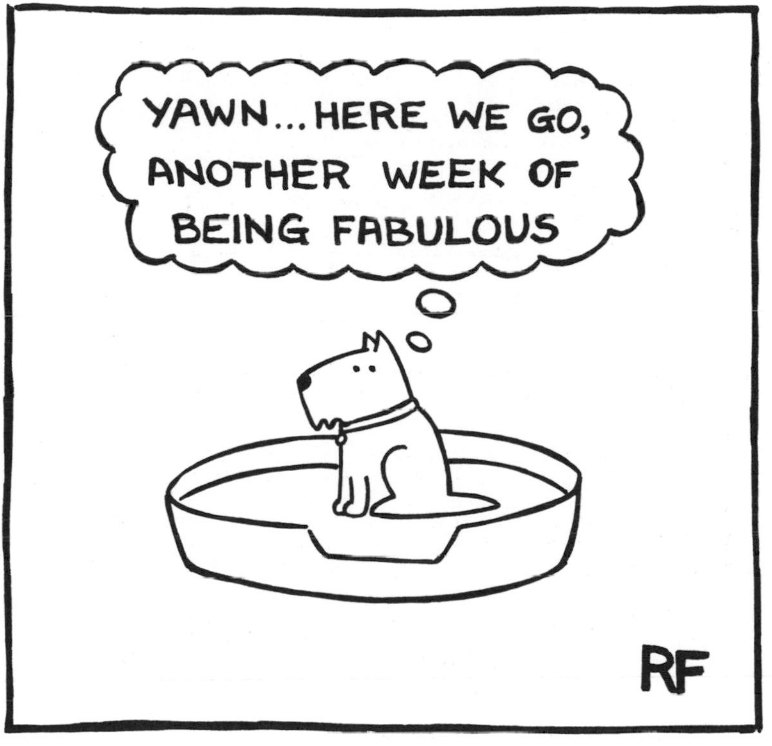
YAWN... HERE WE GO, ANOTHER WEEK OF BEING FABULOUS
RF

AFTER THE STORM...

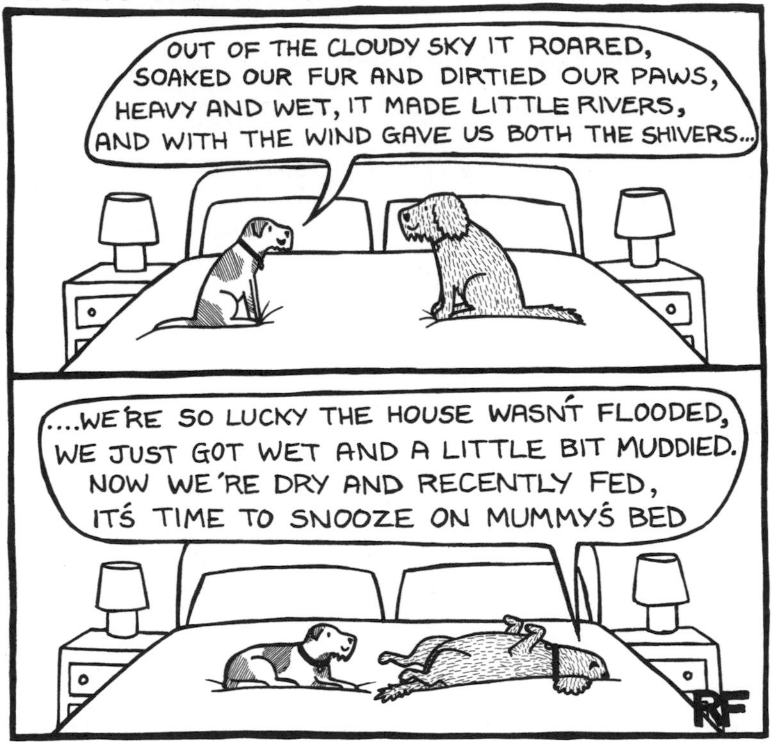

OUT OF THE CLOUDY SKY IT ROARED, SOAKED OUR FUR AND DIRTIED OUR PAWS, HEAVY AND WET, IT MADE LITTLE RIVERS, AND WITH THE WIND GAVE US BOTH THE SHIVERS...
....WE'RE SO LUCKY THE HOUSE WASN'T FLOODED, WE JUST GOT WET AND A LITTLE BIT MUDDIED. NOW WE'RE DRY AND RECENTLY FED, IT'S TIME TO SNOOZE ON MUMMY'S BED
RF

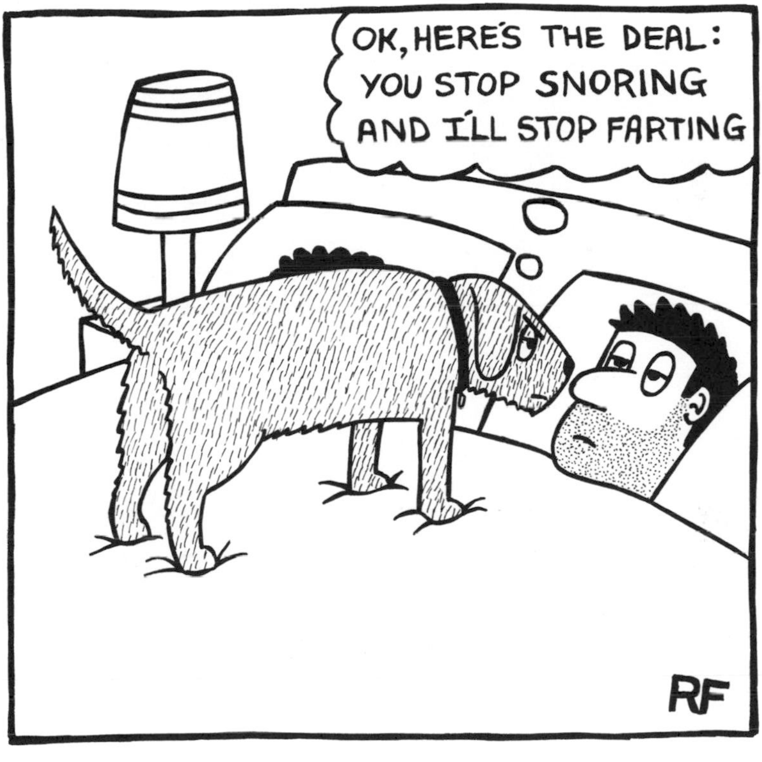
OK, HERE'S THE DEAL: YOU STOP SNORING AND I'LL STOP FARTING
RF

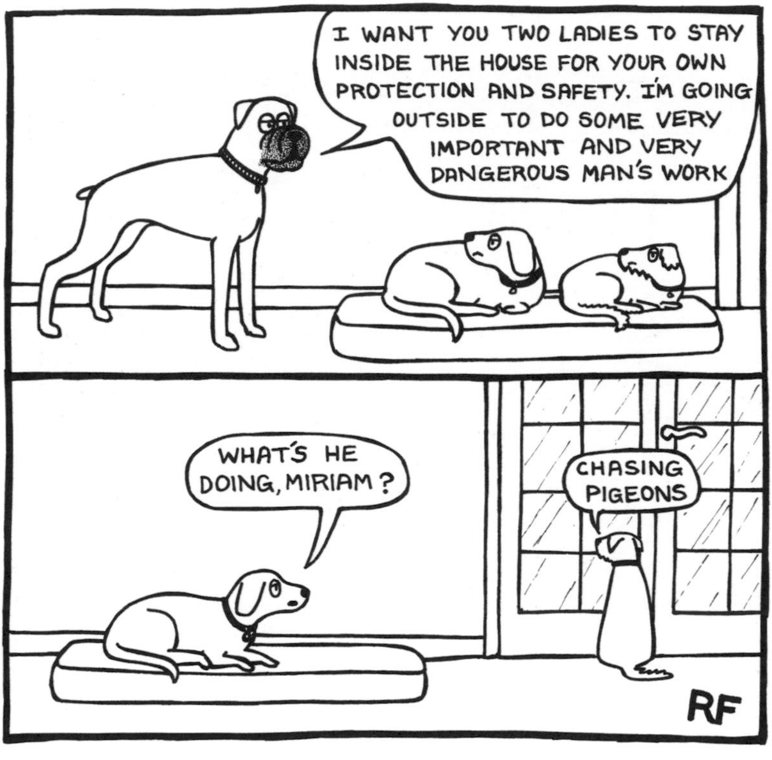
I WANT YOU TWO LADIES TO STAY INSIDE THE HOUSE FOR YOUR OWN PROTECTION AND SAFETY. I'M GOING OUTSIDE TO DO SOME VERY IMPORTANT AND VERY DANGEROUS MAN'S WORK
WHAT'S HE DOING, MIRIAM?
CHASING PIGEONS
RF

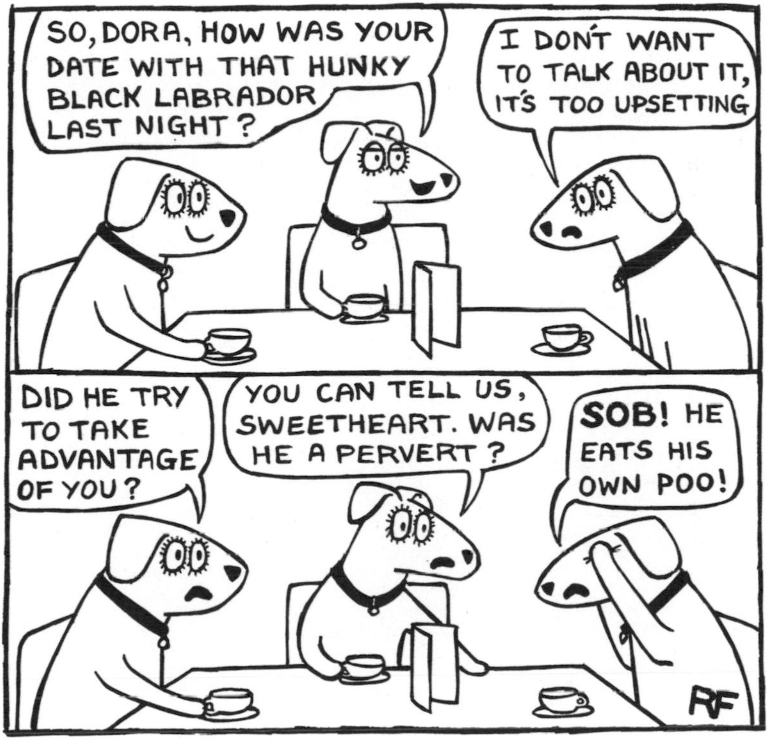
SO, DORA, HOW WAS YOUR DATE WITH THAT HUNKY BLACK LABRADOR LAST NIGHT ?
I DON'T WANT TO TALK ABOUT IT, IT'S TOO UPSETTING
DID HE TRY TO TAKE ADVANTAGE OF YOU ?
YOU CAN TELL US, SWEETHEART. WAS HE A PERVERT ?
SOB! HE EATS HIS OWN POO!
RF

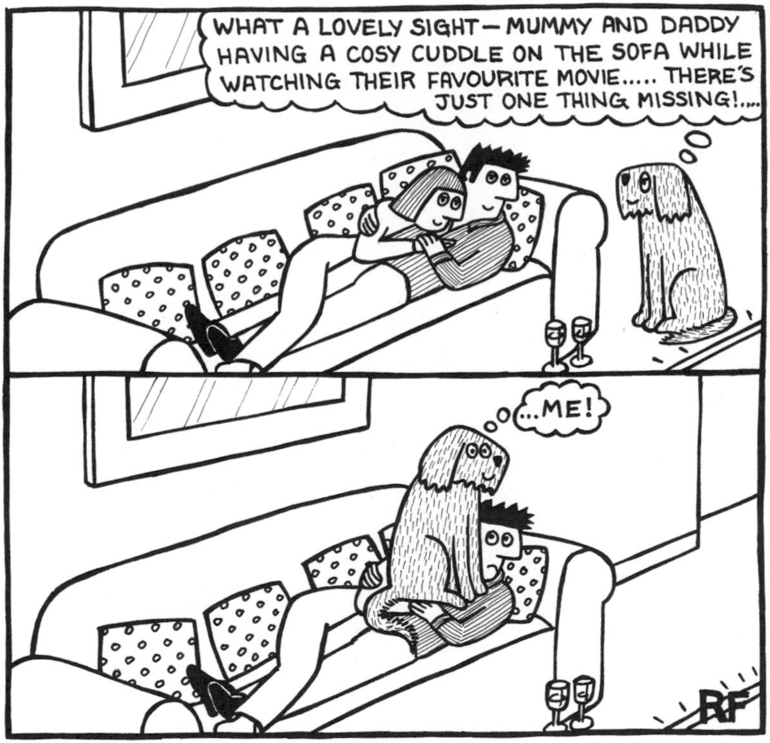
WHAT A LOVELY SIGHT — MUMMY AND DADDY HAVING A COSY CUDDLE ON THE SOFA WHILE WATCHING THEIR FAVOURITE MOVIE..... THERE'S JUST ONE THING MISSING!....
...ME!
RF

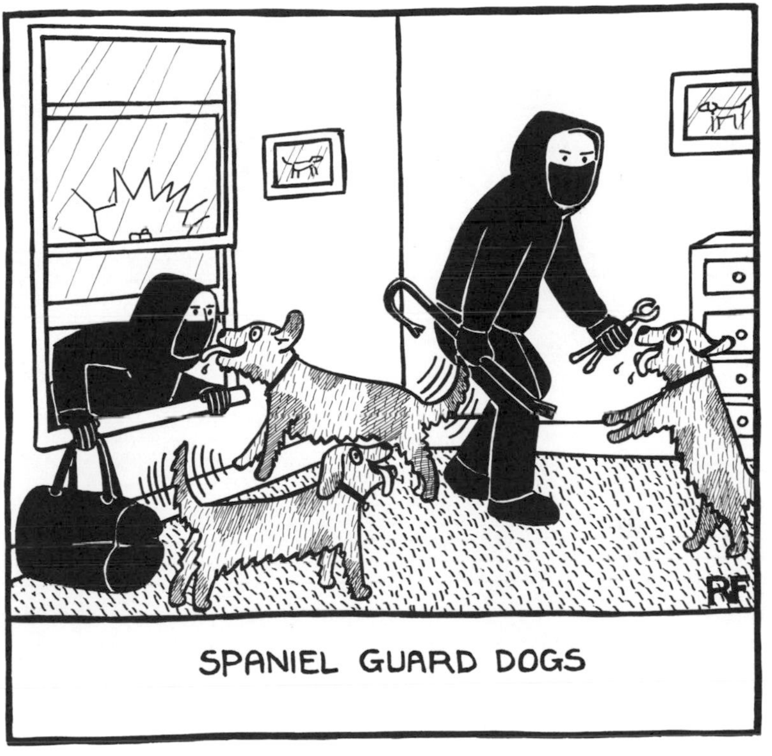
RF

SPANIEL GUARD DOGS

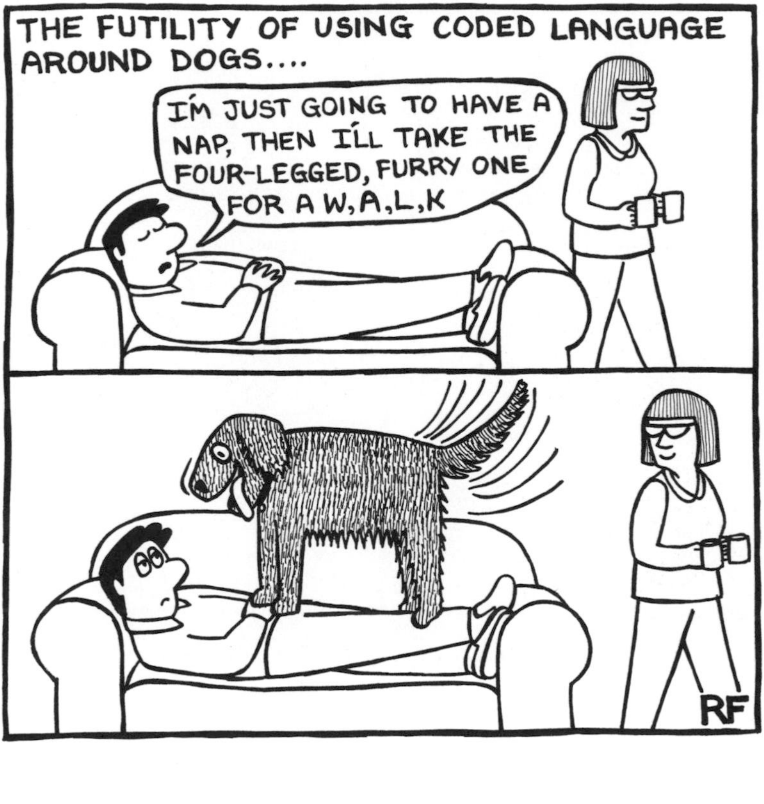
THE FUTILITY OF USING CODED LANGUAGE AROUND DOGS....
I'M JUST GOING TO HAVE A NAP, THEN I'LL TAKE THE FOUR-LEGGED, FURRY ONE FOR A W,A,L,K
RF

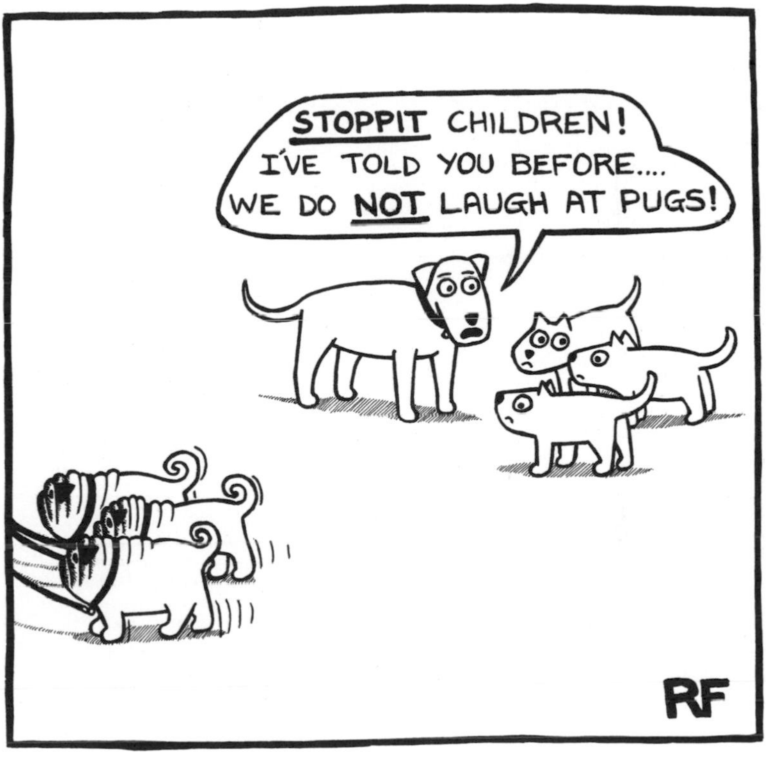
STOPPIT CHILDREN! I'VE TOLD YOU BEFORE.... WE DO NOT LAUGH AT PUGS!
RF

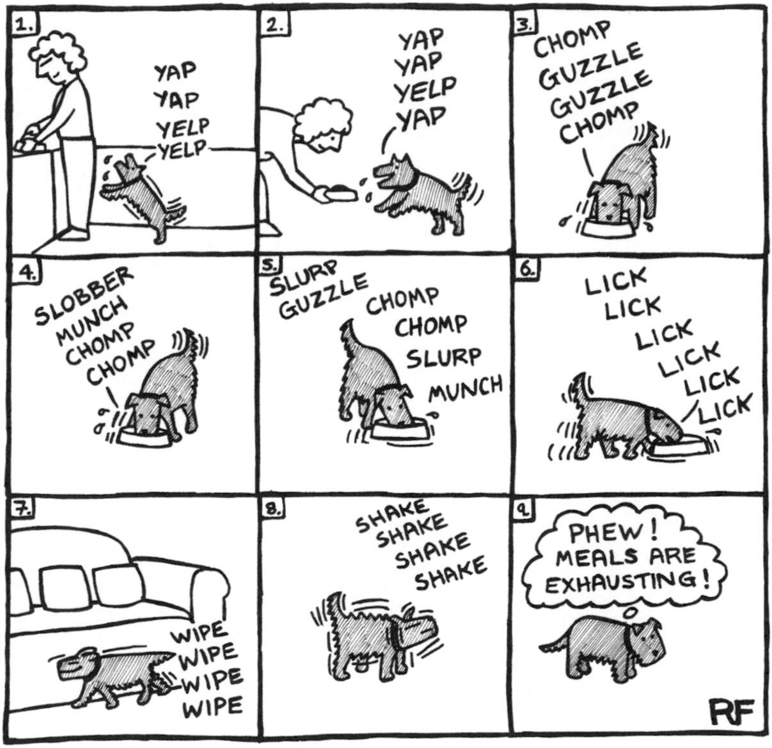
1.
YAP
YAP
YELP
YELP
2.
YAP
YAP
YELP
YAP
3.
CHOMP
GUZZLE
GUZZLE
CHOMP
4.
SLOBBER
MUNCH
CHOMP
CHOMP
5.
SLURP
GUZZLE
CHOMP
CHOMP
SLURP
MUNCH
6.
LICK
LICK
LICK
LICK
LICK
LICK
7.
WIPE
WIPE
WIPE
WIPE
8.
SHAKE
SHAKE
SHAKE
SHAKE
9.
PHEW! MEALS ARE EXHAUSTING!
RF

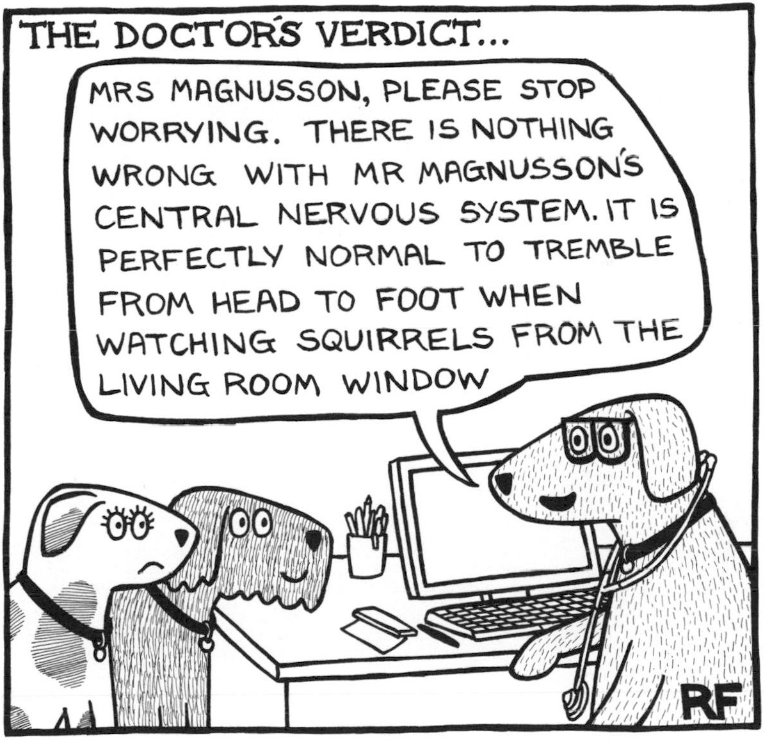
THE DOCTOR'S VERDICT...
MRS MAGNUSSON, PLEASE STOP WORRYING. THERE IS NOTHING WRONG WITH MR MAGNUSSON'S CENTRAL NERVOUS SYSTEM. IT IS PERFECTLY NORMAL TO TREMBLE FROM HEAD TO FOOT WHEN WATCHING SQUIRRELS FROM THE LIVING ROOM WINDOW
RF

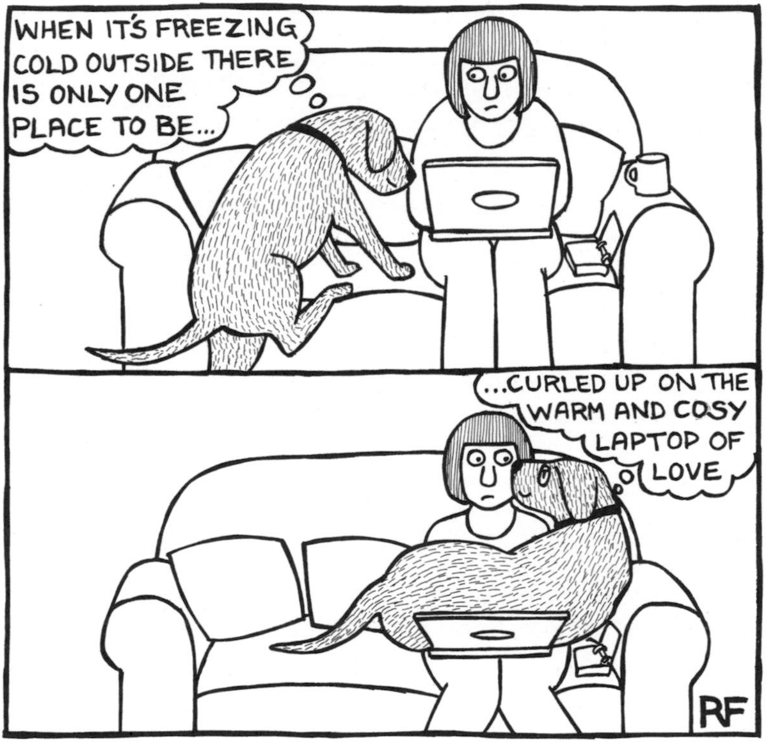
WHEN IT'S FREEZING COLD OUTSIDE THERE IS ONLY ONE PLACE TO BE...
...CURLED UP ON THE WARM AND COSY LAPTOP OF LOVE
RF

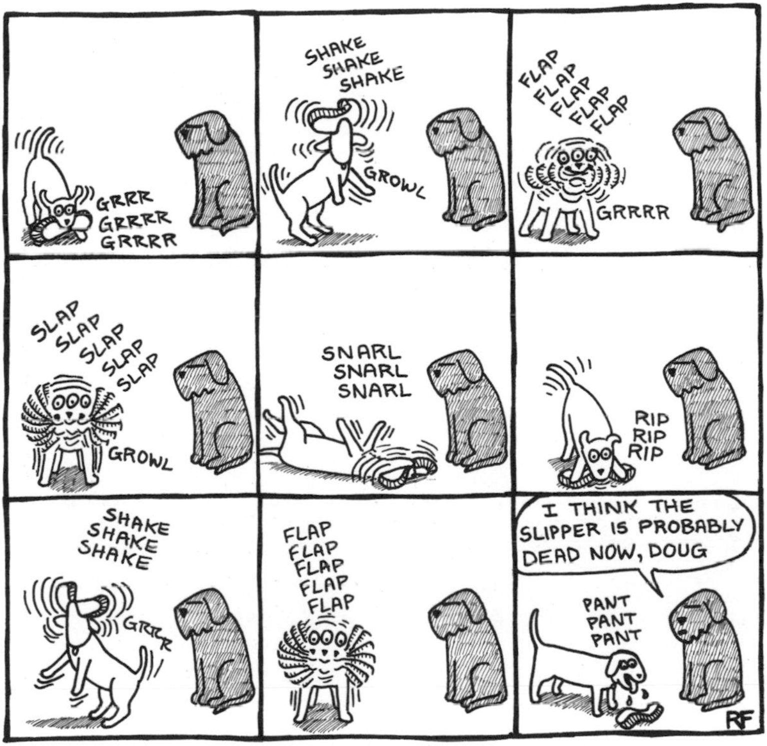
GRRR
GRRRR
GRRRR
SHAKE
SHAKE
SHAKE
GROWL
FLAP
FLAP
FLAP
FLAP
FLAP
GRRRR
SLAP
SLAP
SLAP
SLAP
SLAP
GROWL
SNARL
SNARL
SNARL
RIP
RIP
RIP
SHAKE
SHAKE
SHAKE
GRRR
FLAP
FLAP
FLAP
FLAP
FLAP
I THINK THE SLIPPER IS PROBABLY DEAD NOW, DOUG
PANT
PANT
PANT
RF

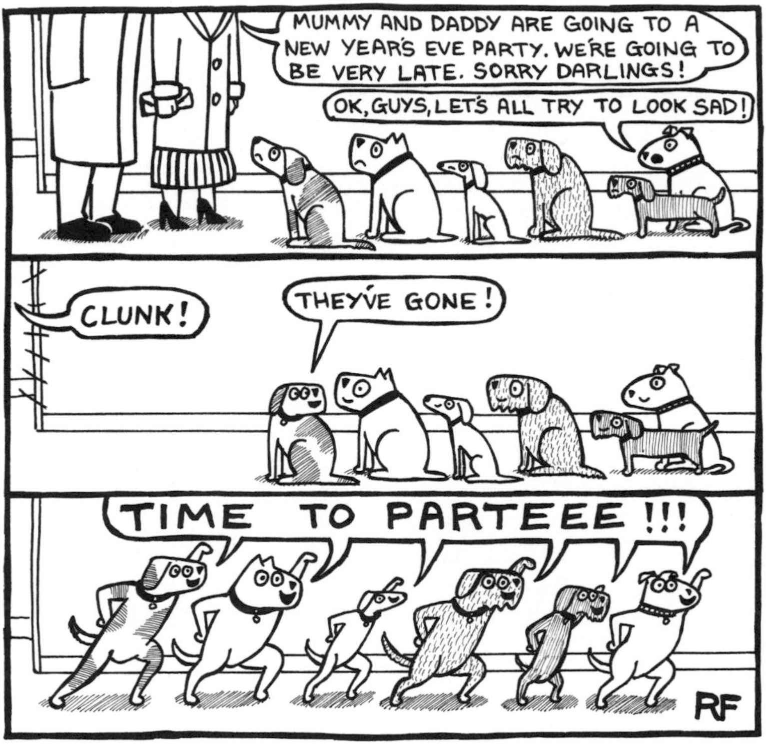

MUMMY AND DADDY ARE GOING TO A NEW YEAR'S EVE PARTY. WE'RE GOING TO BE VERY LATE. SORRY DARLINGS!
OK, GUYS, LET'S ALL TRY TO LOOK SAD!
CLUNK!
THEY'VE GONE!
TIME TO PARTEEE!!!
RF

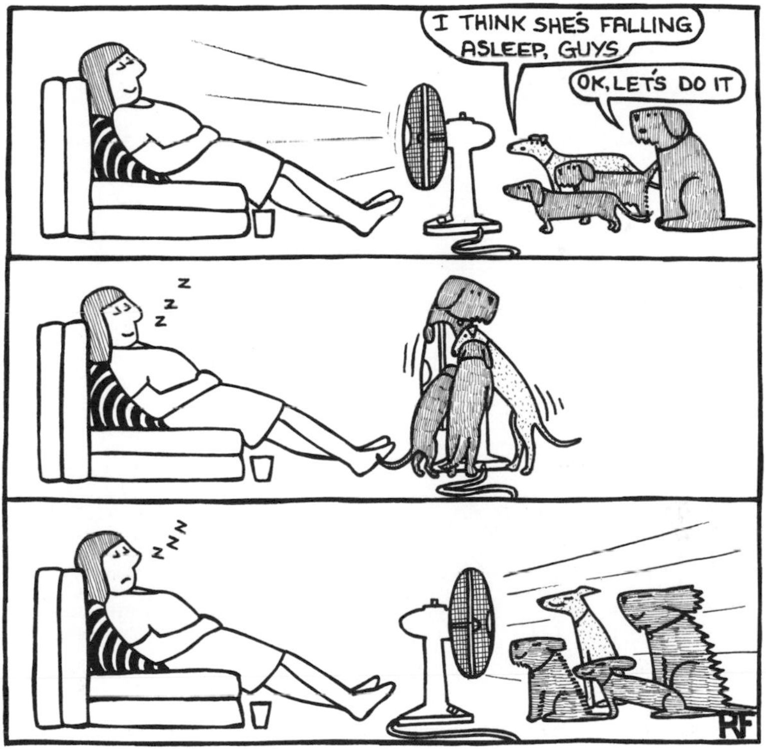
I THINK SHE'S FALLING ASLEEP, GUYS
OK, LET'S DO IT
Z Z Z
Z Z Z
RF

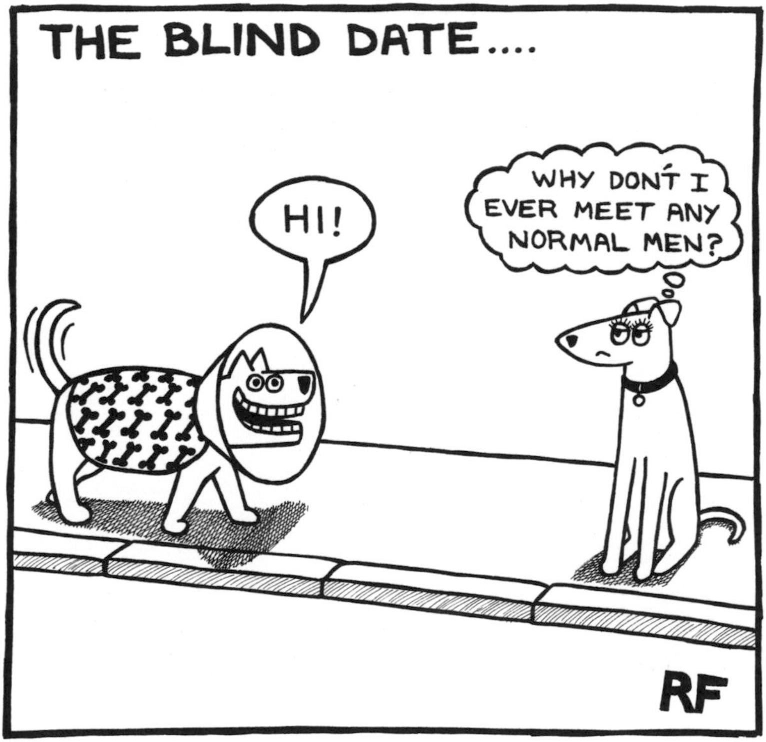
THE BLIND DATE....
HI!
WHY DON'T I EVER MEET ANY NORMAL MEN?
RF

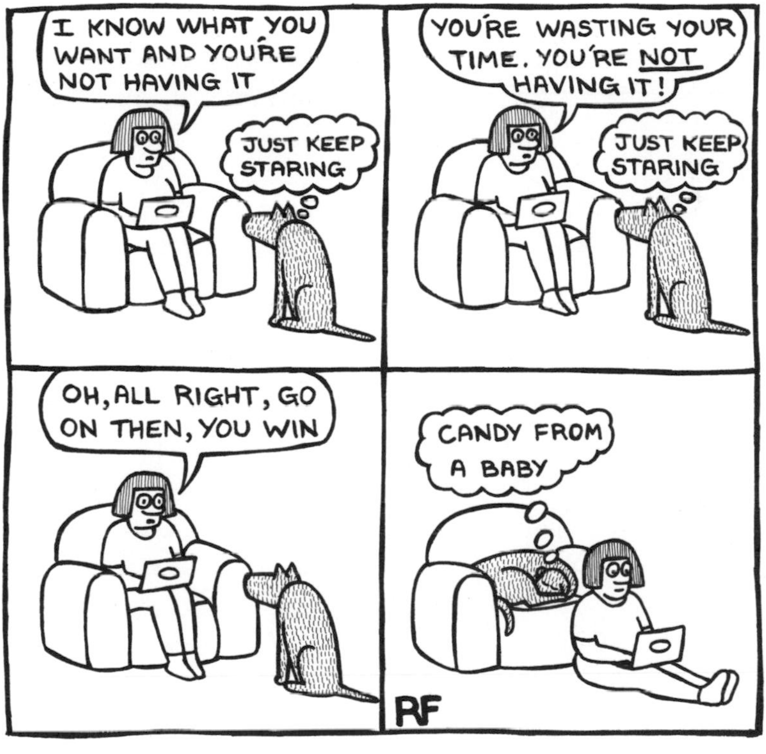
I KNOW WHAT YOU WANT AND YOU'RE NOT HAVING IT
JUST KEEP STARING
YOU'RE WASTING YOUR TIME. YOU'RE NOT HAVING IT!
JUST KEEP STARING
OH, ALL RIGHT, GO ON THEN, YOU WIN
CANDY FROM A BABY
RF

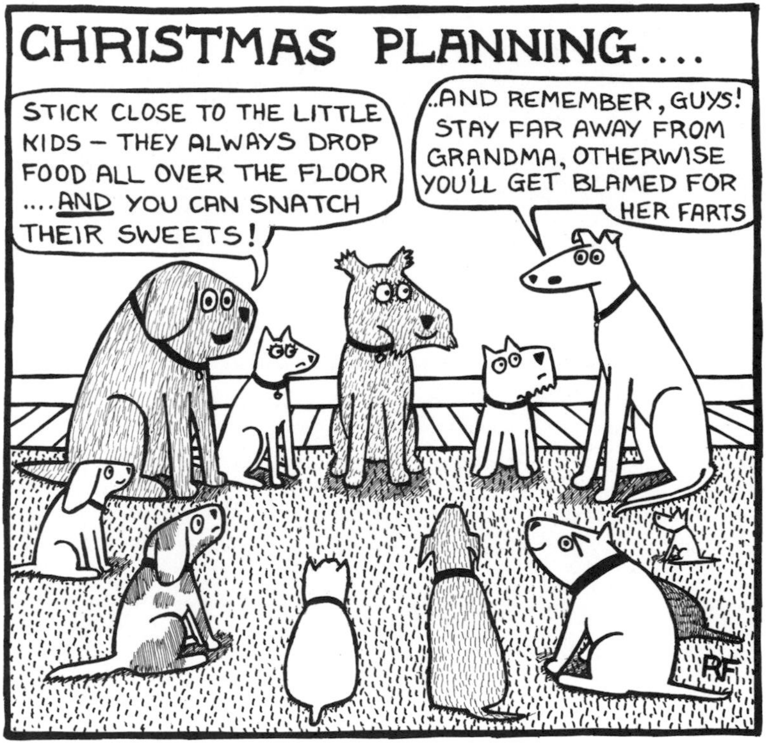
CHRISTMAS PLANNING....
STICK CLOSE TO THE LITTLE KIDS – THEY ALWAYS DROP FOOD ALL OVER THE FLOOR ....AND YOU CAN SNATCH THEIR SWEETS!
..AND REMEMBER, GUYS! STAY FAR AWAY FROM GRANDMA, OTHERWISE YOU'LL GET BLAMED FOR HER FARTS
RF

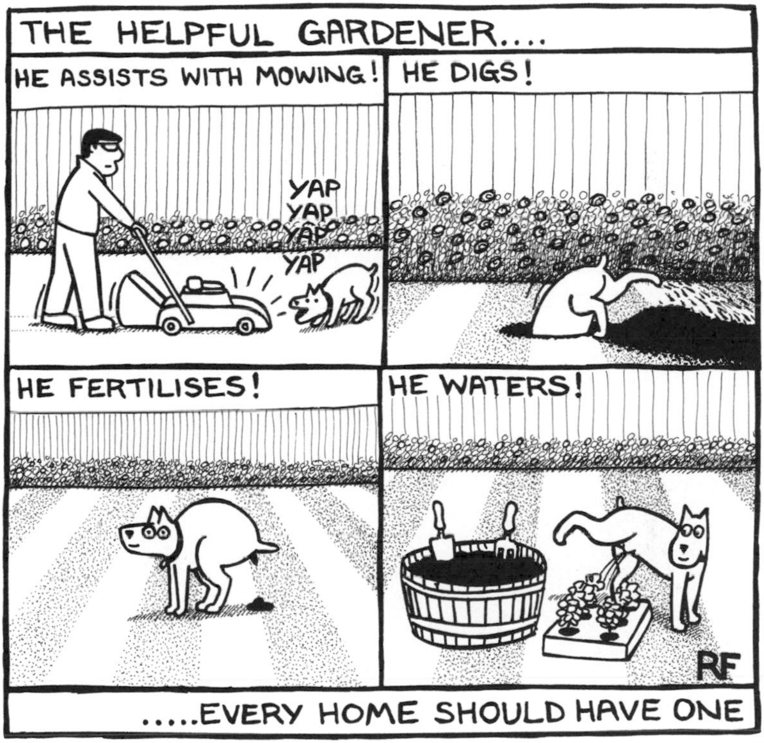
THE HELPFUL GARDENER....
HE ASSISTS WITH MOWING!
YAP YAP YAP YAP
HE DIGS!
HE FERTILISES!
HE WATERS!
RF
.....EVERY HOME SHOULD HAVE ONE

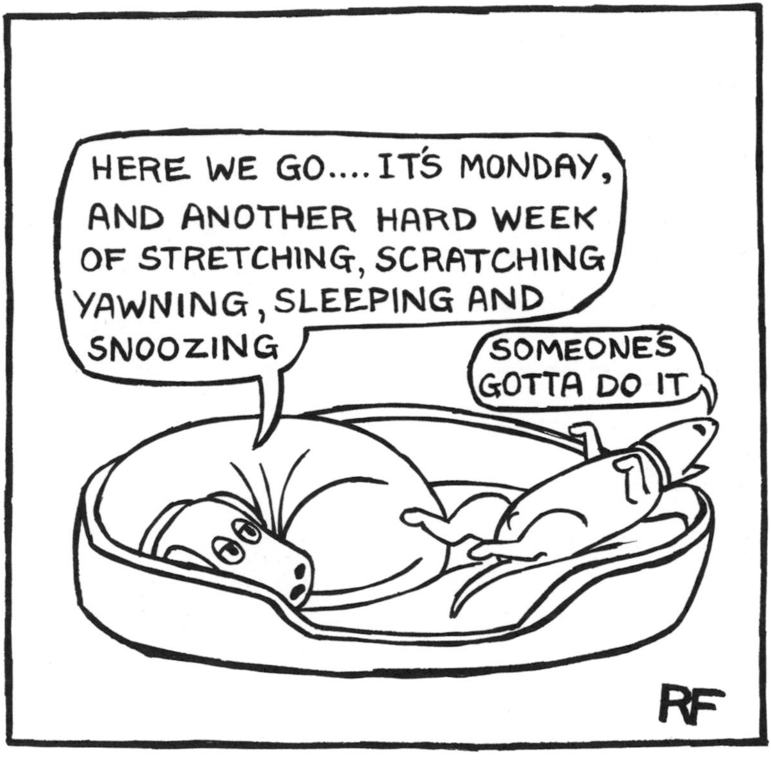
HERE WE GO.... IT'S MONDAY, AND ANOTHER HARD WEEK OF STRETCHING, SCRATCHING YAWNING, SLEEPING AND SNOOZING
SOMEONE'S GOTTA DO IT
RF

AT PUPPY HIGH SCHOOL...
SILENT BUT DEADLY FART EXAMINATION
PFFT!
I'M SORRY YOUNG MAN, BUT WE ALL HEARD THAT. YOU'LL HAVE TO RETURN NEXT SEMESTER AND TAKE THE EXAM AGAIN
SILENT BUT DEADLY FART EXAMINATION
RF

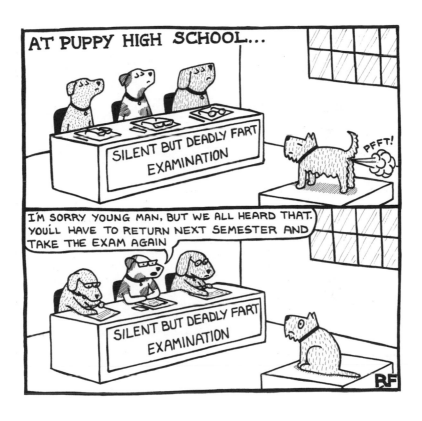

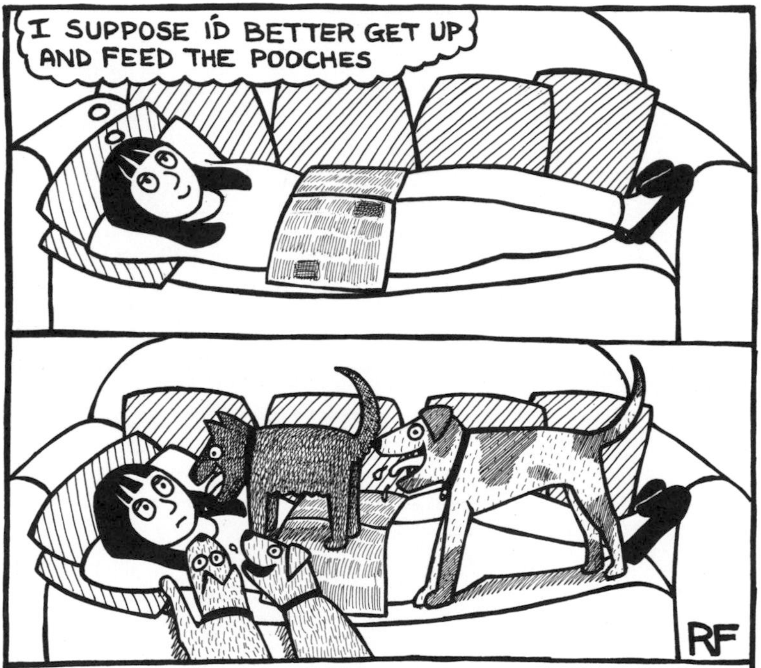
I SUPPOSE I'D BETTER GET UP AND FEED THE POOCHES
RF

PSYCHIC DOGS

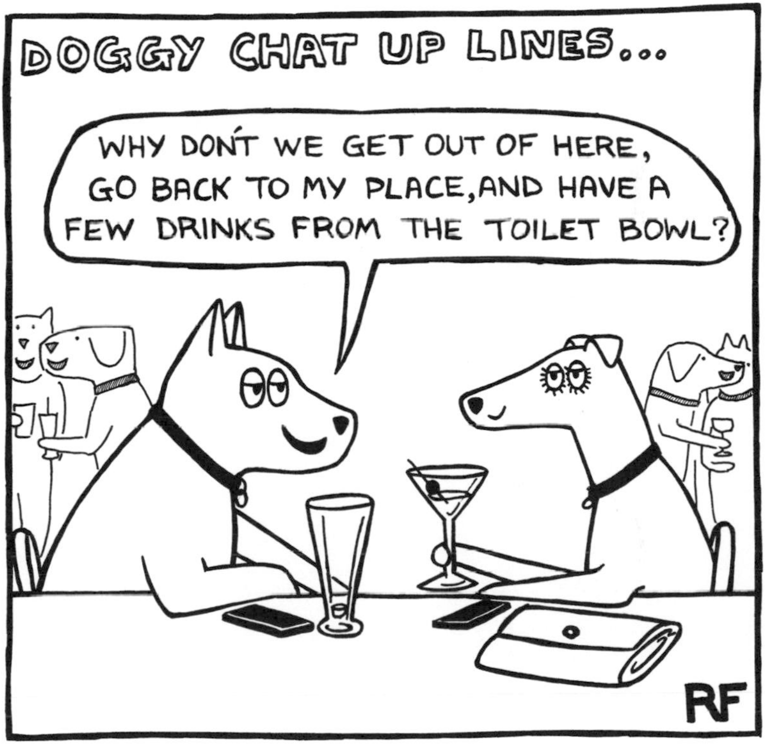
DOGGY CHAT UP LINES...
WHY DON'T WE GET OUT OF HERE, GO BACK TO MY PLACE, AND HAVE A FEW DRINKS FROM THE TOILET BOWL?
RF

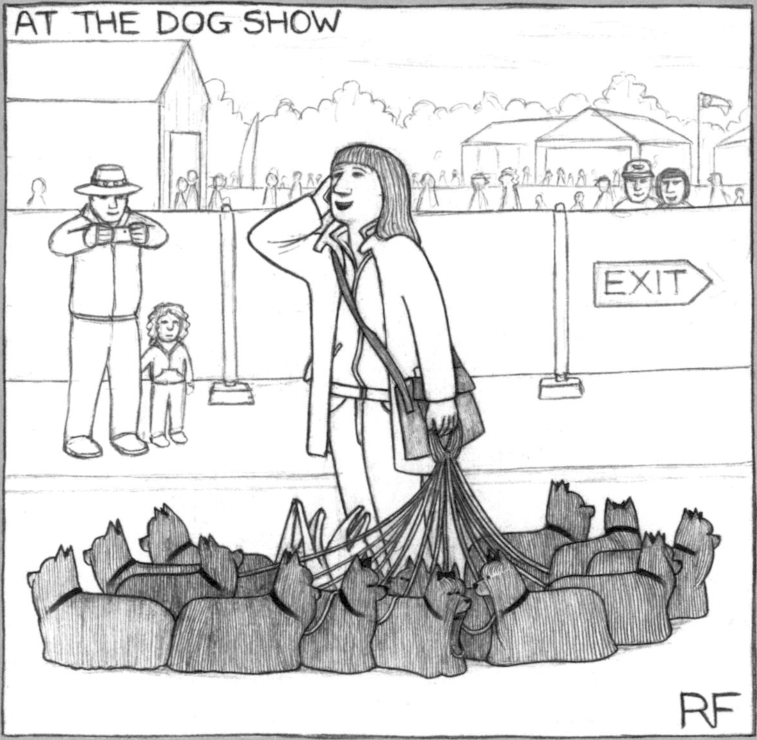
AT THE DOG SHOW
EXIT
RF

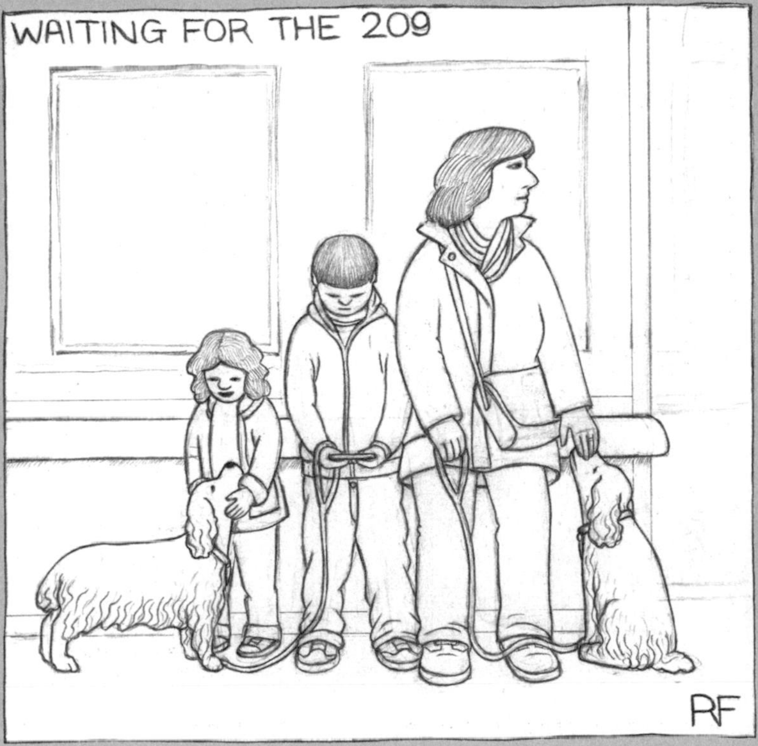
WAITING FOR THE 209
RF

REMEMBER SEX?
VAGUELY
RF

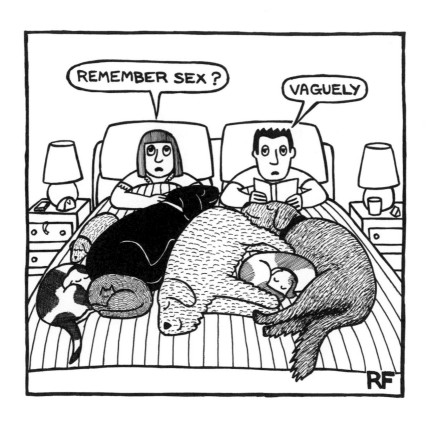

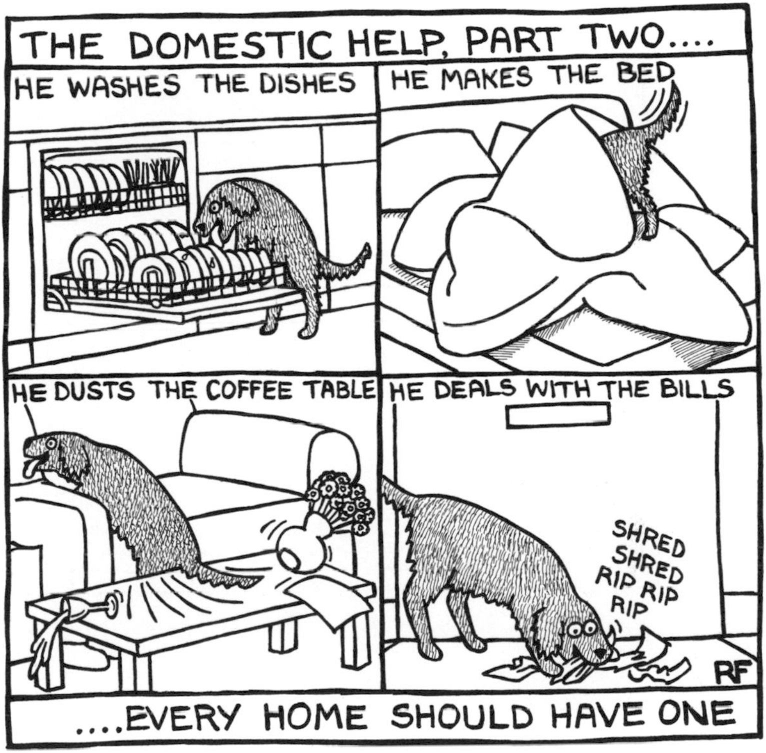
THE DOMESTIC HELP, PART TWO....
HE WASHES THE DISHES
HE MAKES THE BED
HE DUSTS THE COFFEE TABLE
HE DEALS WITH THE BILLS
SHRED
SHRED
RIP RIP
RIP
RF
....EVERY HOME SHOULD HAVE ONE

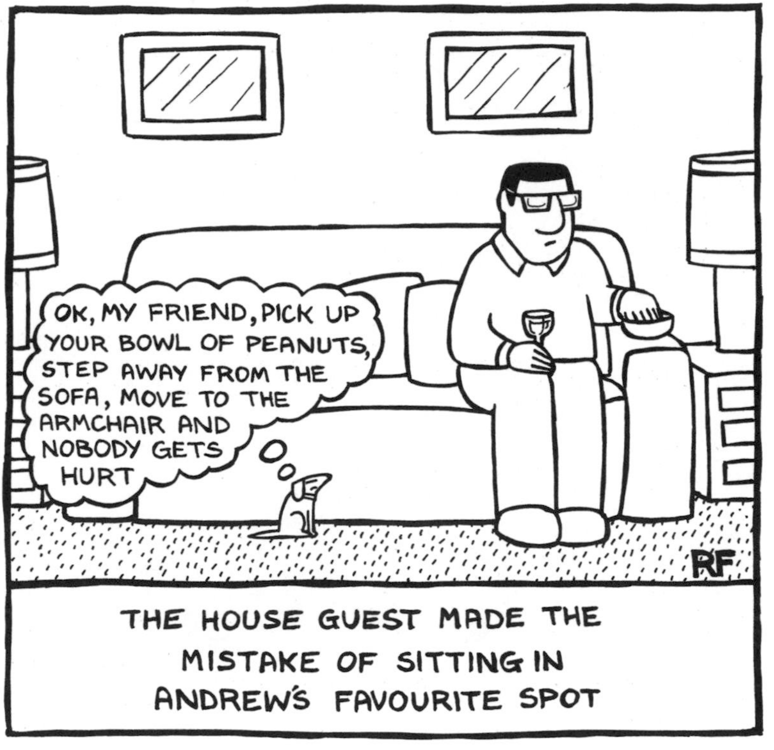
OK, MY FRIEND, PICK UP YOUR BOWL OF PEANUTS, STEP AWAY FROM THE SOFA, MOVE TO THE ARMCHAIR AND NOBODY GETS HURT
RF

THE HOUSE GUEST MADE THE MISTAKE OF SITTING IN ANDREW'S FAVOURITE SPOT

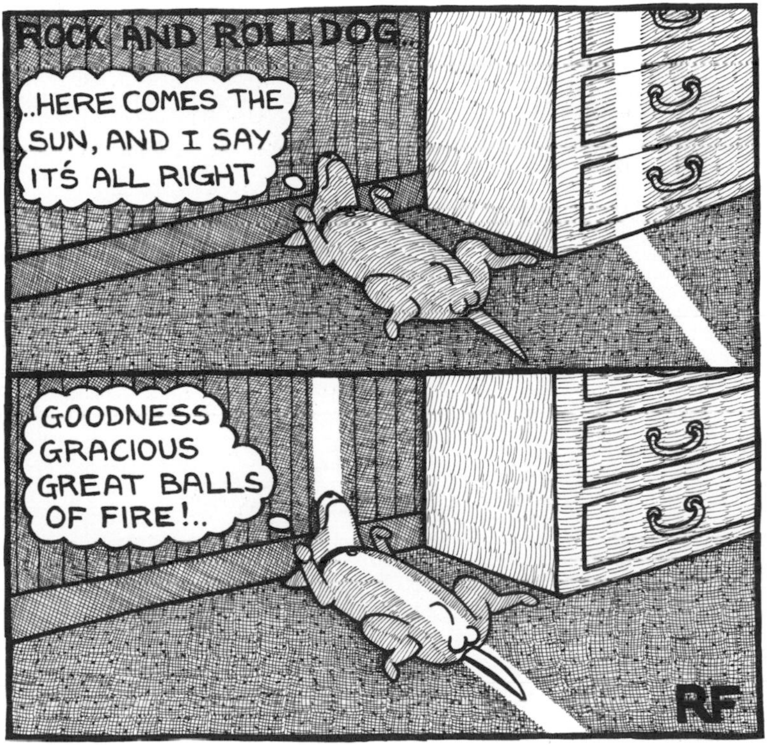
ROCK AND ROLL DOG..
..HERE COMES THE SUN, AND I SAY IT'S ALL RIGHT
GOODNESS GRACIOUS GREAT BALLS OF FIRE!..
RF

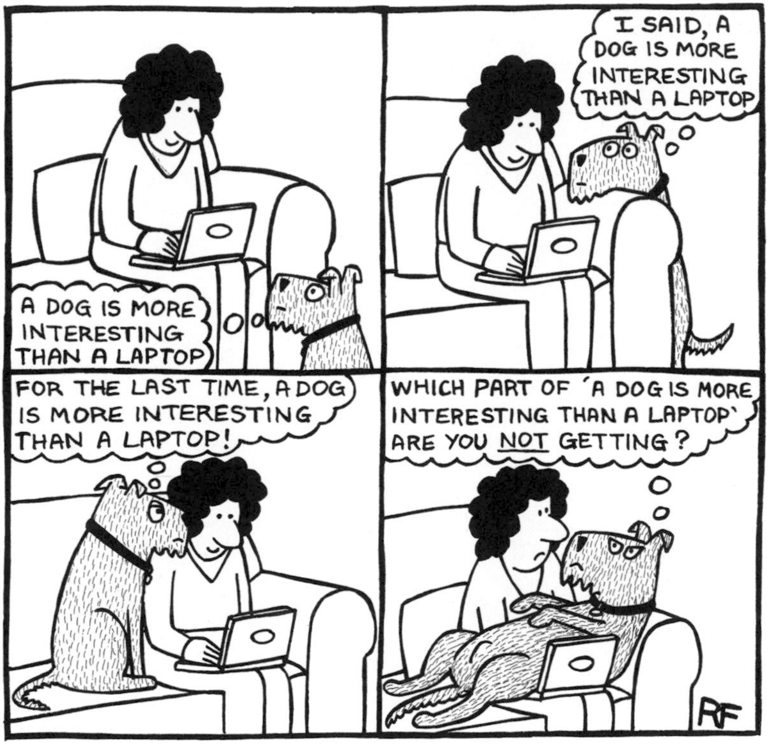
A DOG IS MORE INTERESTING THAN A LAPTOP
I SAID, A DOG IS MORE INTERESTING THAN A LAPTOP
FOR THE LAST TIME, A DOG IS MORE INTERESTING THAN A LAPTOP!
WHICH PART OF 'A DOG IS MORE INTERESTING THAN A LAPTOP' ARE YOU NOT GETTING?
RF

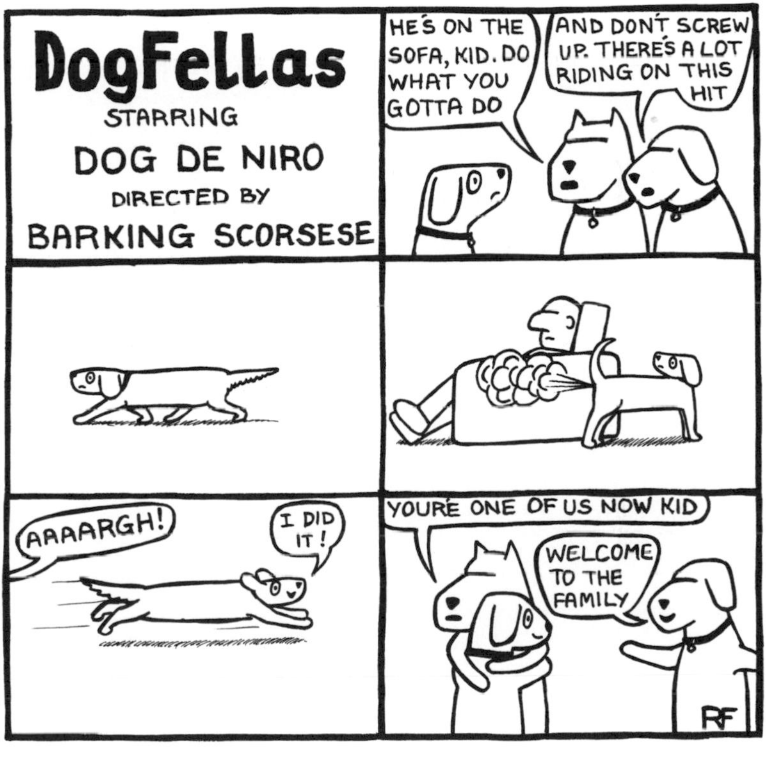
DogFellas
STARRING
DOG DE NIRO
DIRECTED BY
BARKING SCORSESE
HE'S ON THE SOFA, KID. DO WHAT YOU GOTTA DO
AND DON'T SCREW UP. THERE'S A LOT RIDING ON THIS HIT
AAAARGH!
I DID IT!
YOU'RE ONE OF US NOW KID
WELCOME TO THE FAMILY
RF

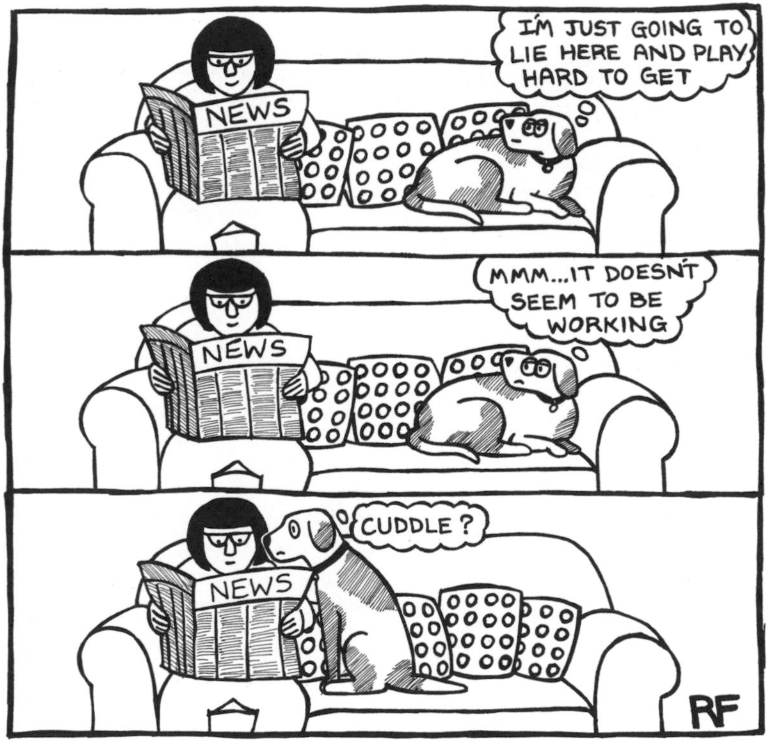
I'M JUST GOING TO LIE HERE AND PLAY HARD TO GET
NEWS
MMM...IT DOESN'T SEEM TO BE WORKING
NEWS
CUDDLE?
NEWS
RF

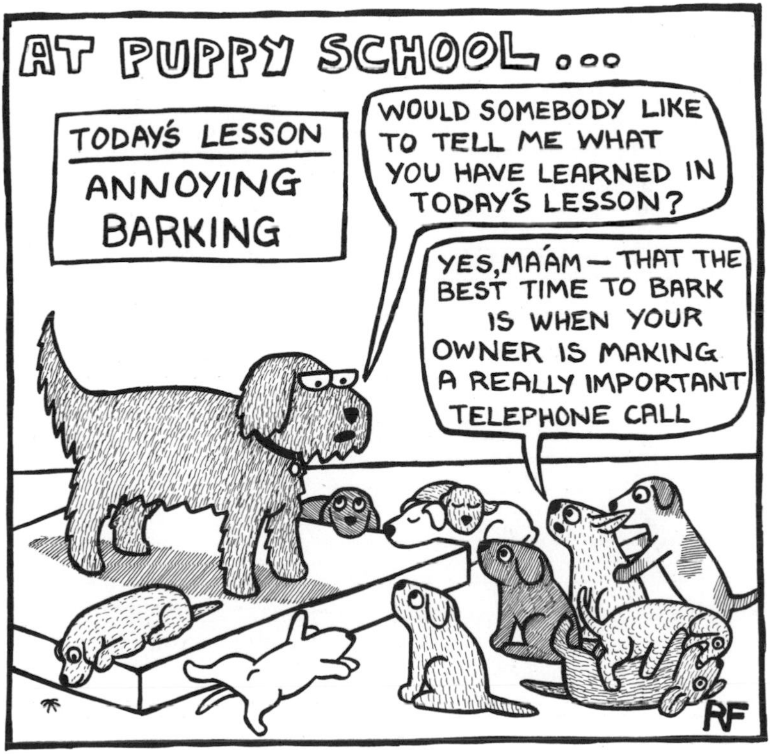
AT PUPPY SCHOOL...
TODAY'S LESSON
ANNOYING BARKING
WOULD SOMEBODY LIKE TO TELL ME WHAT YOU HAVE LEARNED IN TODAY'S LESSON?
YES, MA'AM — THAT THE BEST TIME TO BARK IS WHEN YOUR OWNER IS MAKING A REALLY IMPORTANT TELEPHONE CALL
RF

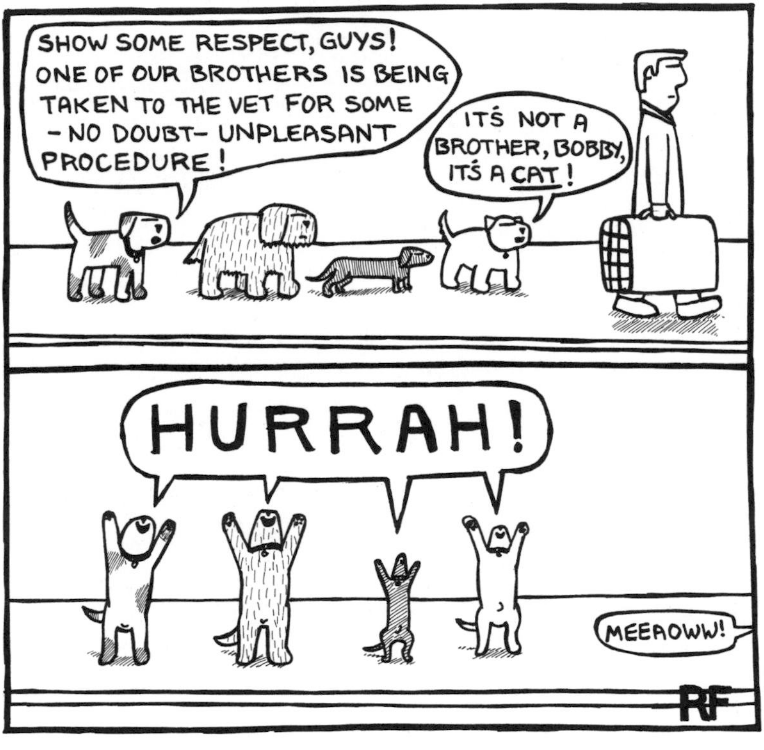
SHOW SOME RESPECT, GUYS! ONE OF OUR BROTHERS IS BEING TAKEN TO THE VET FOR SOME - NO DOUBT- UNPLEASANT PROCEDURE!
ITS NOT A BROTHER, BOBBY, ITS A CAT!
HURRAH!
MEEAOWW!
RF

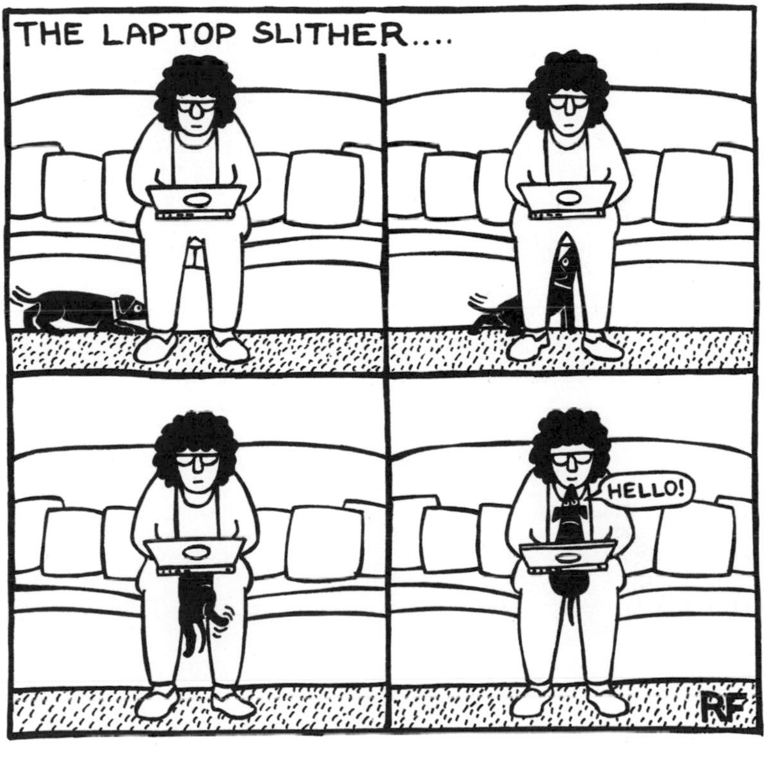
THE LAPTOP SLITHER....
HELLO!
RF

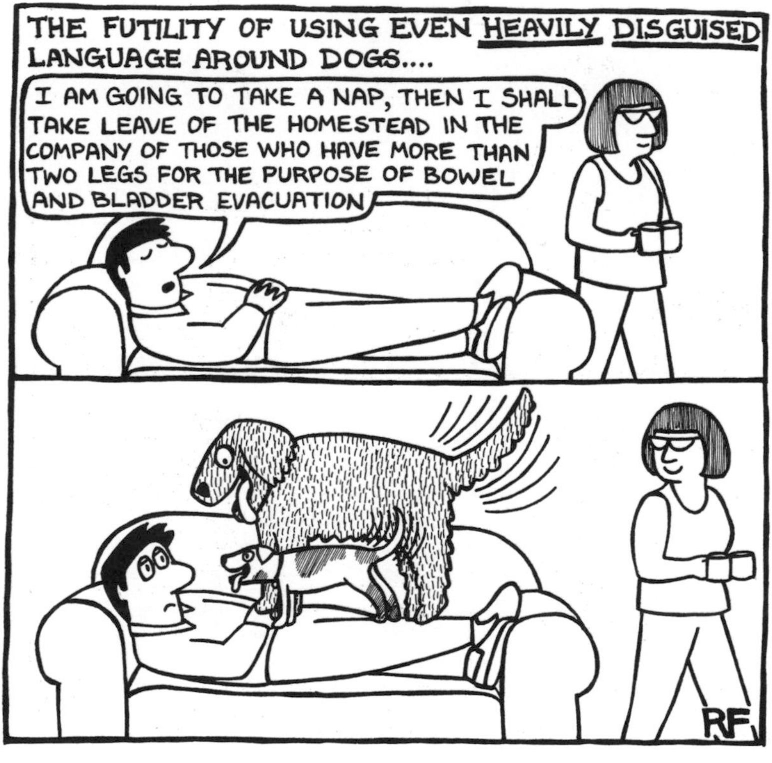
THE FUTILITY OF USING EVEN HEAVILY DISGUISED LANGUAGE AROUND DOGS....
I AM GOING TO TAKE A NAP, THEN I SHALL TAKE LEAVE OF THE HOMESTEAD IN THE COMPANY OF THOSE WHO HAVE MORE THAN TWO LEGS FOR THE PURPOSE OF BOWEL AND BLADDER EVACUATION
RF

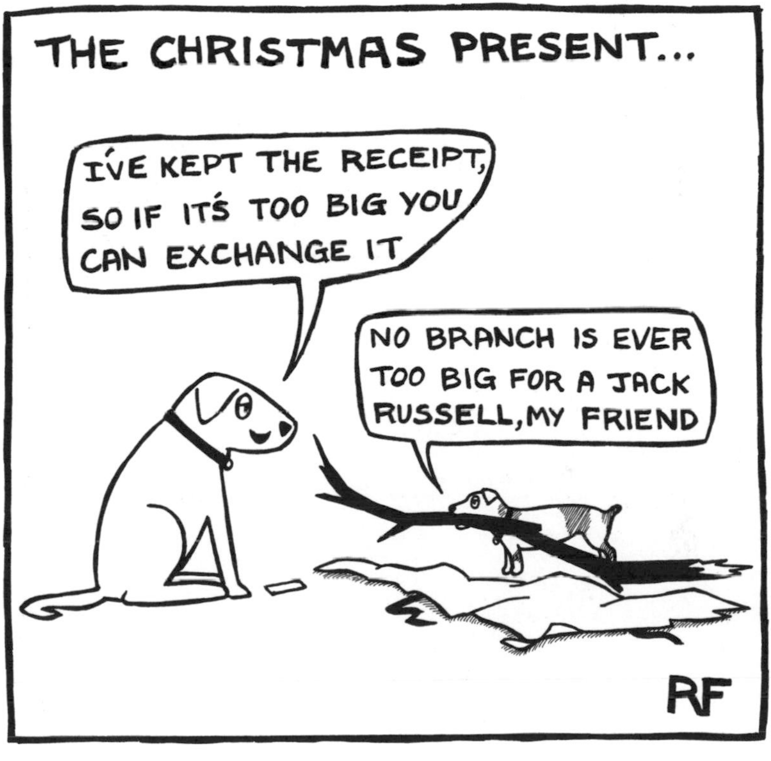
THE CHRISTMAS PRESENT...
I'VE KEPT THE RECEIPT, SO IF IT'S TOO BIG YOU CAN EXCHANGE IT
NO BRANCH IS EVER TOO BIG FOR A JACK RUSSELL, MY FRIEND
RF

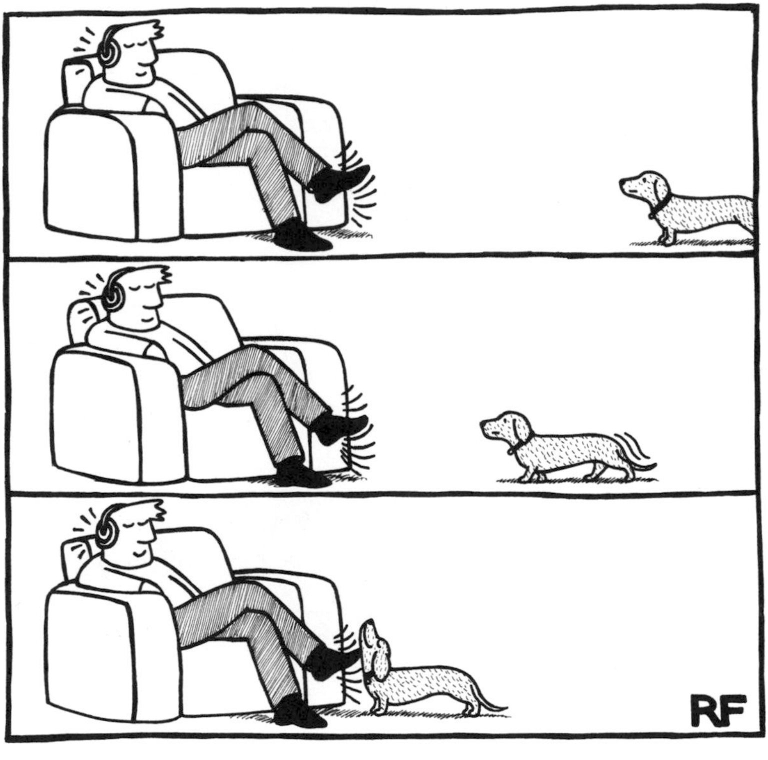
RF

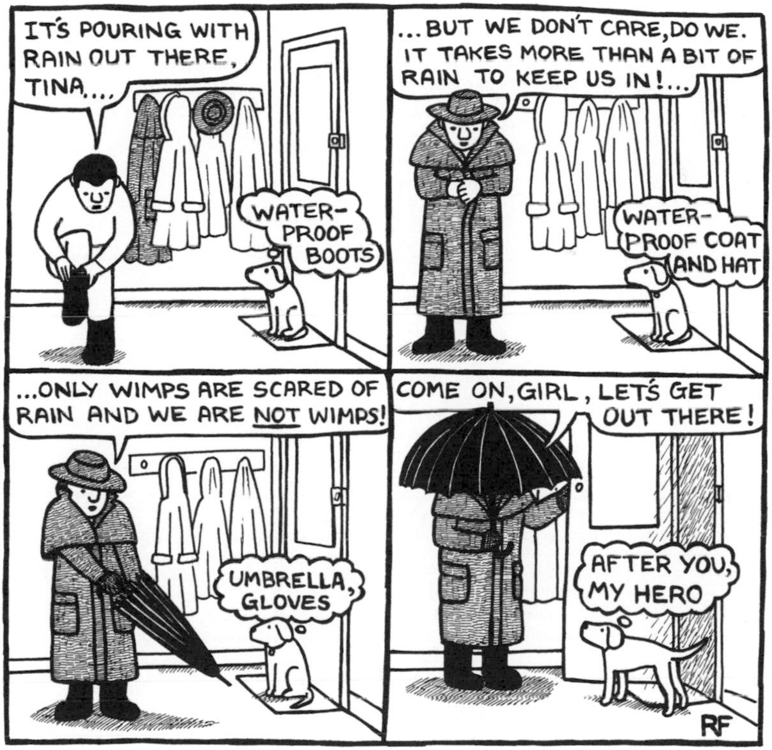
IT'S POURING WITH RAIN OUT THERE, TINA....
WATER-PROOF BOOTS
...BUT WE DON'T CARE, DO WE. IT TAKES MORE THAN A BIT OF RAIN TO KEEP US IN!...
WATER-PROOF COAT AND HAT
...ONLY WIMPS ARE SCARED OF RAIN AND WE ARE NOT WIMPS!
UMBRELLA, GLOVES
COME ON, GIRL, LET'S GET OUT THERE!
AFTER YOU, MY HERO
RF

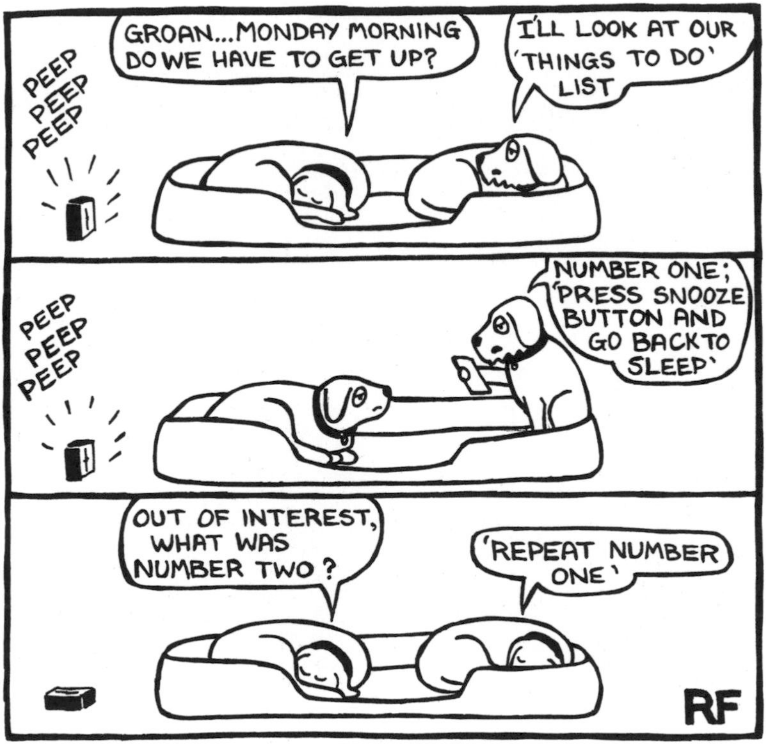
PEEP
PEEP
PEEP
GROAN...MONDAY MORNING DO WE HAVE TO GET UP?
I'LL LOOK AT OUR 'THINGS TO DO' LIST
PEEP
PEEP
PEEP
NUMBER ONE; 'PRESS SNOOZE BUTTON AND GO BACK TO SLEEP'
OUT OF INTEREST, WHAT WAS NUMBER TWO?
'REPEAT NUMBER ONE'
RF

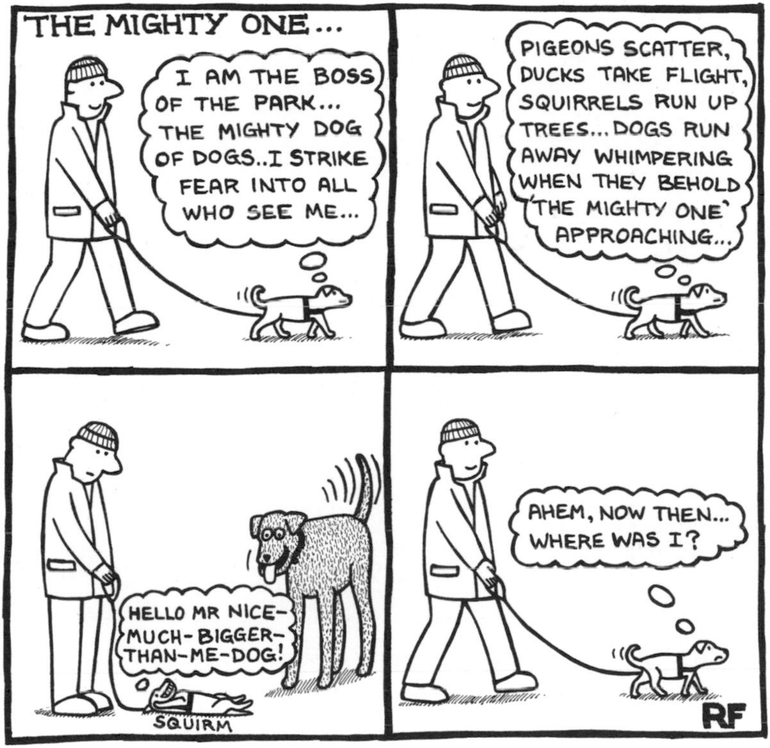
THE MIGHTY ONE...
I AM THE BOSS OF THE PARK... THE MIGHTY DOG OF DOGS..I STRIKE FEAR INTO ALL WHO SEE ME...
PIGEONS SCATTER, DUCKS TAKE FLIGHT, SQUIRRELS RUN UP TREES...DOGS RUN AWAY WHIMPERING WHEN THEY BEHOLD 'THE MIGHTY ONE' APPROACHING...
HELLO MR NICE-MUCH-BIGGER-THAN-ME-DOG!
SQUIRM
AHEM, NOW THEN... WHERE WAS I?
RF

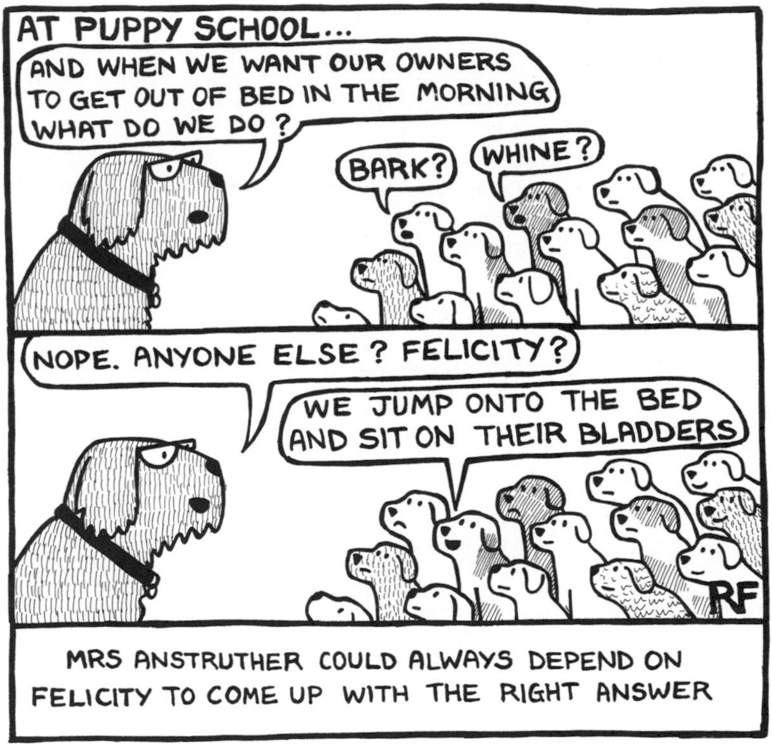
AT PUPPY SCHOOL...
AND WHEN WE WANT OUR OWNERS TO GET OUT OF BED IN THE MORNING WHAT DO WE DO?
BARK?
WHINE?
NOPE. ANYONE ELSE? FELICITY?
WE JUMP ONTO THE BED AND SIT ON THEIR BLADDERS
RF
MRS ANSTRUTHER COULD ALWAYS DEPEND ON FELICITY TO COME UP WITH THE RIGHT ANSWER

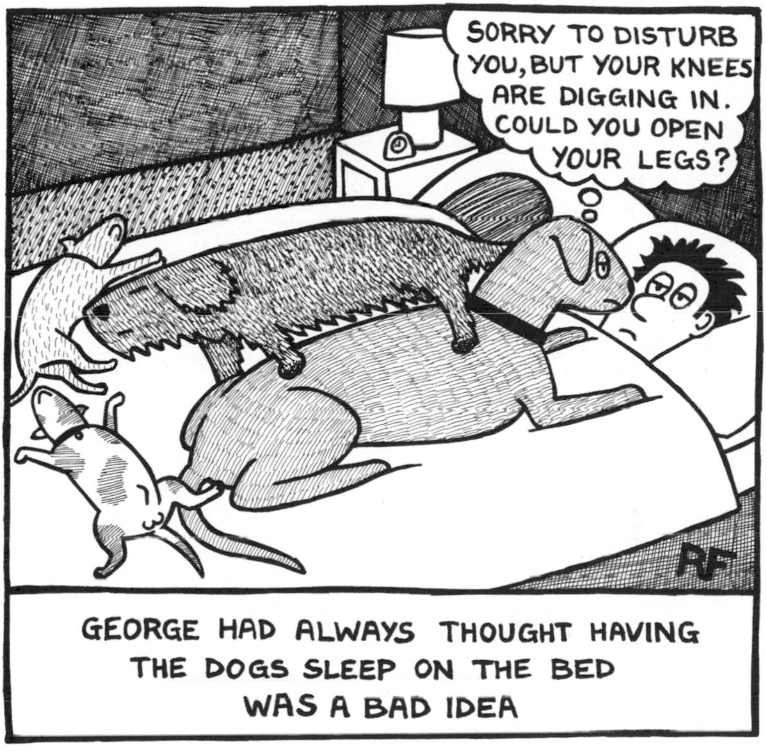
SORRY TO DISTURB YOU, BUT YOUR KNEES ARE DIGGING IN. COULD YOU OPEN YOUR LEGS?
RF

GEORGE HAD ALWAYS THOUGHT HAVING THE DOGS SLEEP ON THE BED WAS A BAD IDEA

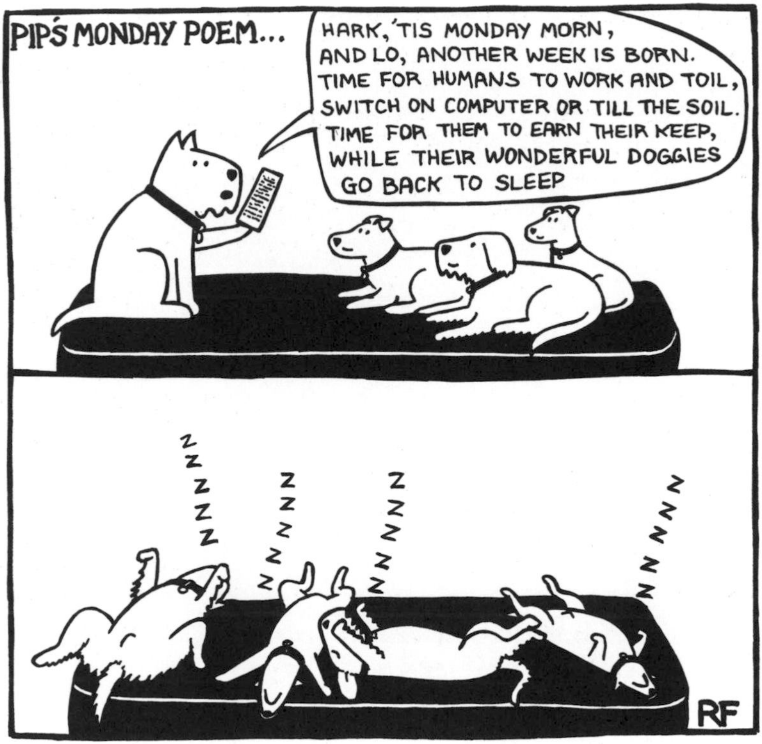
PIP'S MONDAY POEM...
HARK, 'TIS MONDAY MORN, AND LO, ANOTHER WEEK IS BORN. TIME FOR HUMANS TO WORK AND TOIL, SWITCH ON COMPUTER OR TILL THE SOIL. TIME FOR THEM TO EARN THEIR KEEP, WHILE THEIR WONDERFUL DOGGIES GO BACK TO SLEEP
ZZZZZZ
ZZZZZZ
ZZZZZZZ
ZZZZZZZ
RF

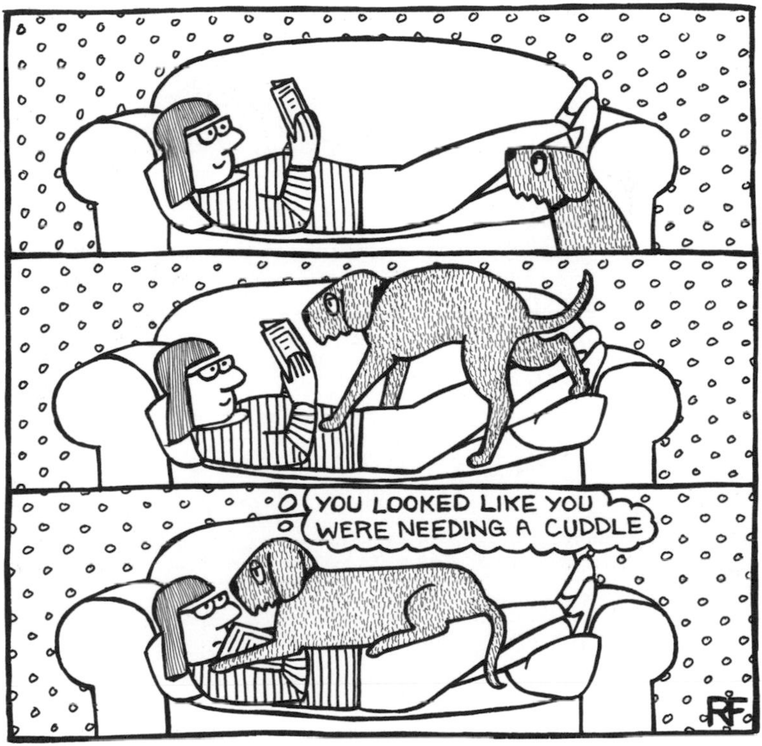
YOU LOOKED LIKE YOU WERE NEEDING A CUDDLE
RF

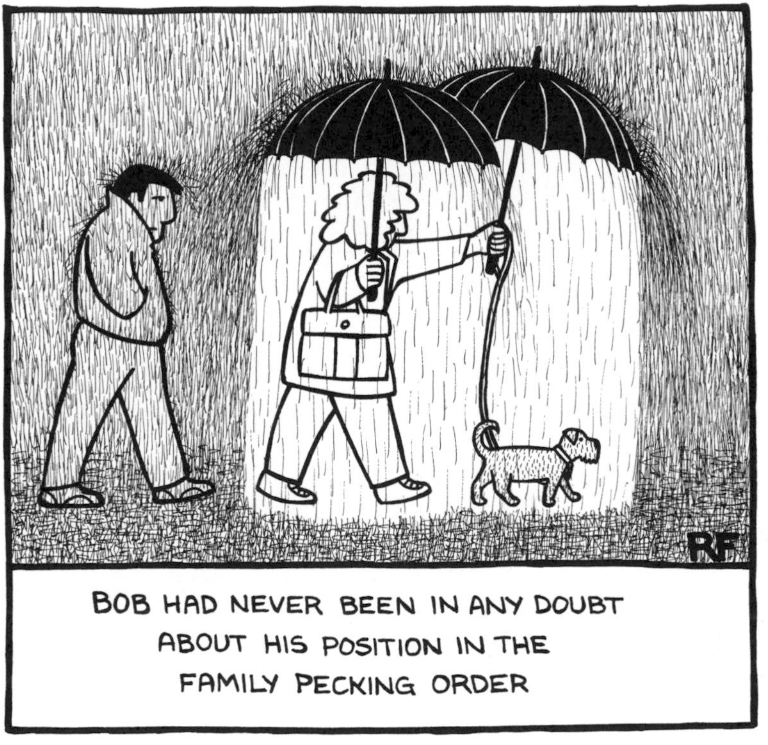
RF

BOB HAD NEVER BEEN IN ANY DOUBT ABOUT HIS POSITION IN THE FAMILY PECKING ORDER

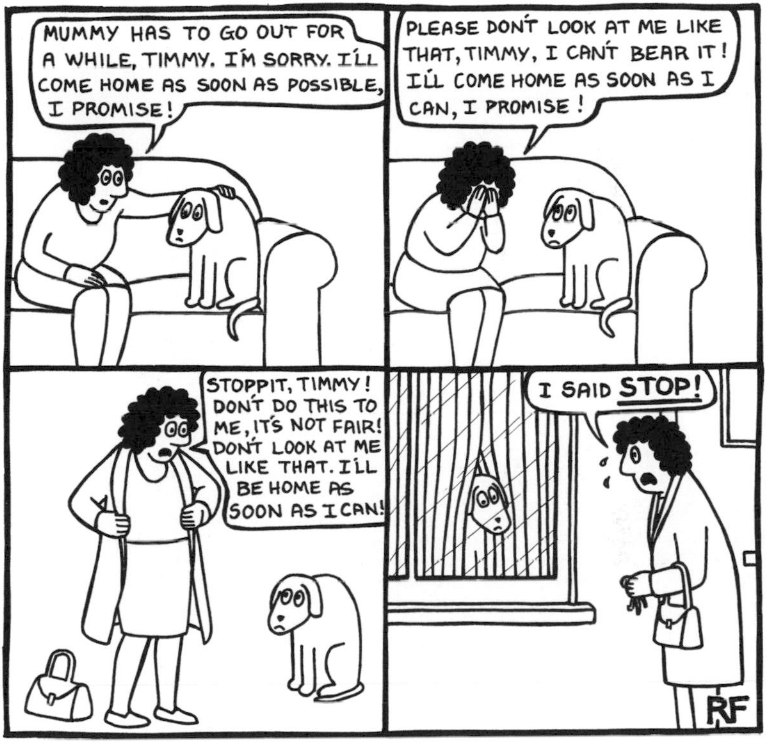
MUMMY HAS TO GO OUT FOR A WHILE, TIMMY. I'M SORRY. I'LL COME HOME AS SOON AS POSSIBLE, I PROMISE!
PLEASE DON'T LOOK AT ME LIKE THAT, TIMMY, I CAN'T BEAR IT! I'LL COME HOME AS SOON AS I CAN, I PROMISE!
STOPPIT, TIMMY! DON'T DO THIS TO ME, IT'S NOT FAIR! DON'T LOOK AT ME LIKE THAT. I'LL BE HOME AS SOON AS I CAN!
I SAID STOP!
RF

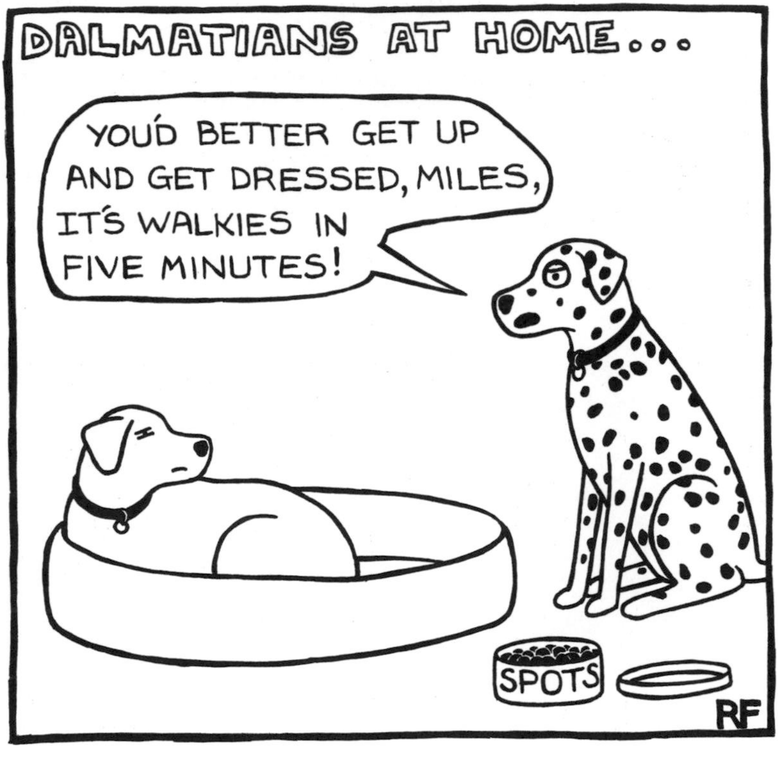
DALMATIANS AT HOME...
YOU'D BETTER GET UP AND GET DRESSED, MILES, IT'S WALKIES IN FIVE MINUTES!
SPOTS
RF

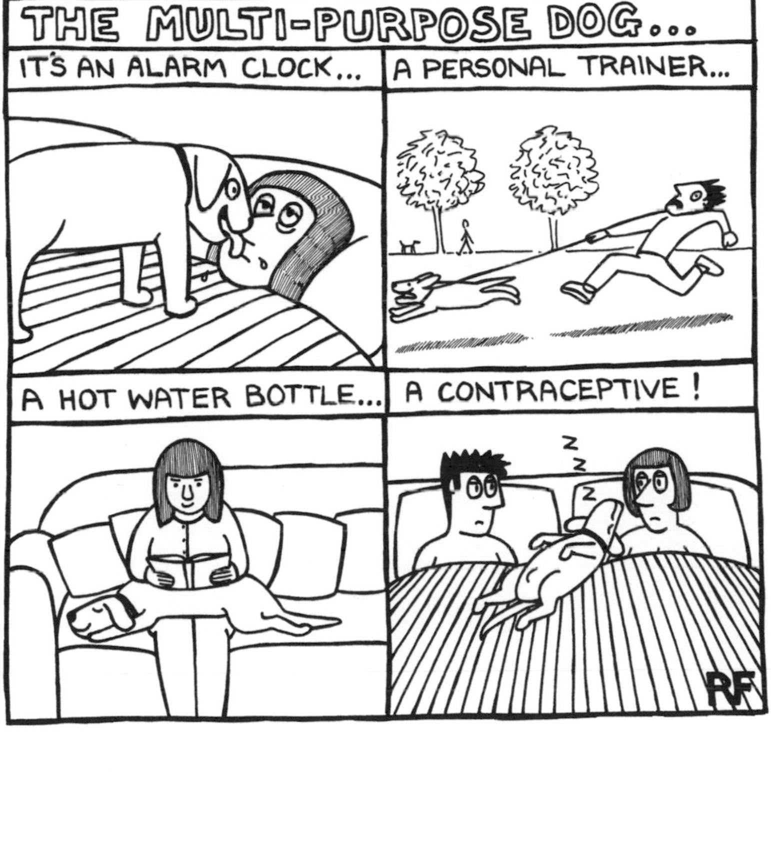
THE MULTI-PURPOSE DOG...
IT'S AN ALARM CLOCK...
A PERSONAL TRAINER...
A HOT WATER BOTTLE...
A CONTRACEPTIVE!
Z
Z
Z
RF

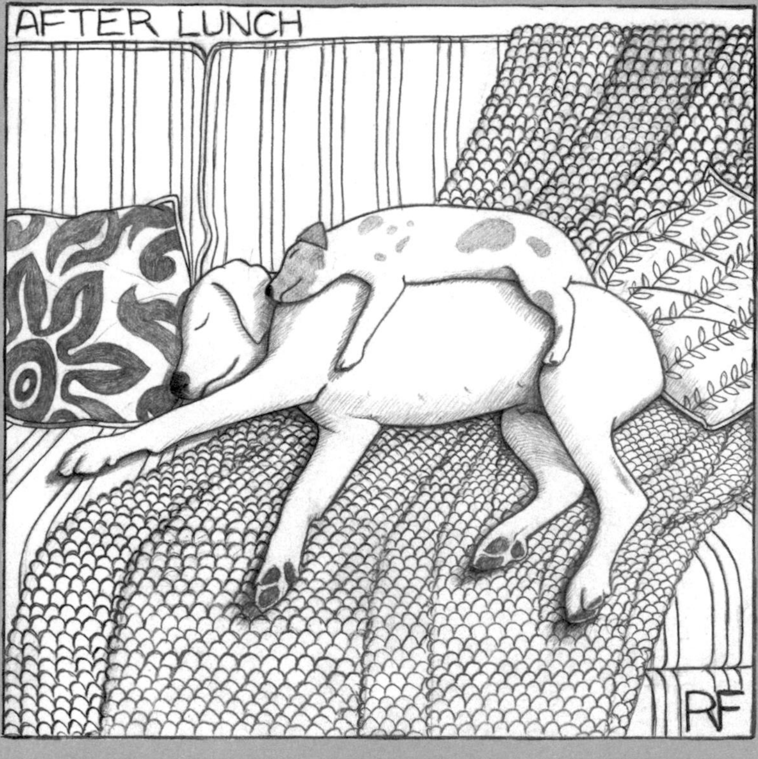
AFTER LUNCH
RF

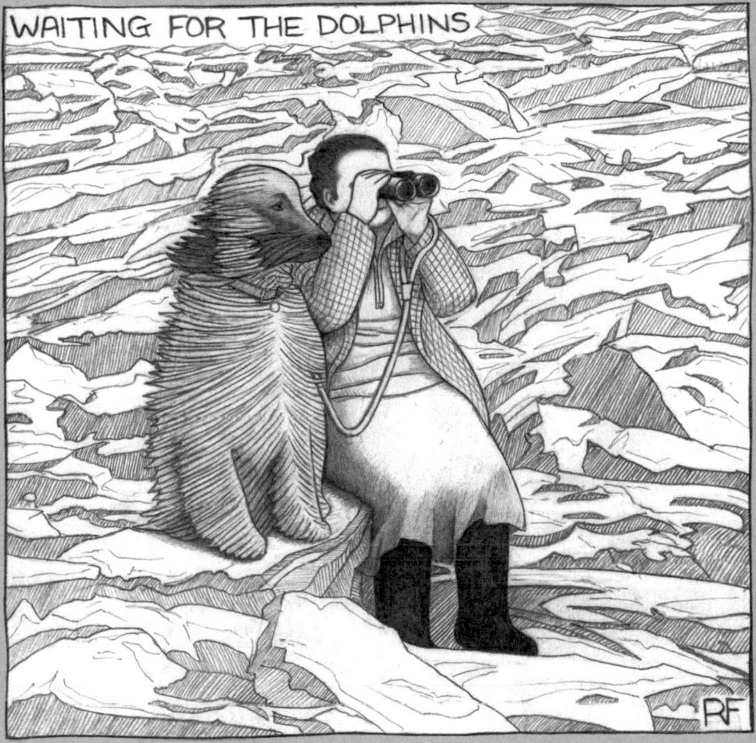
WAITING FOR THE DOLPHINS
RF

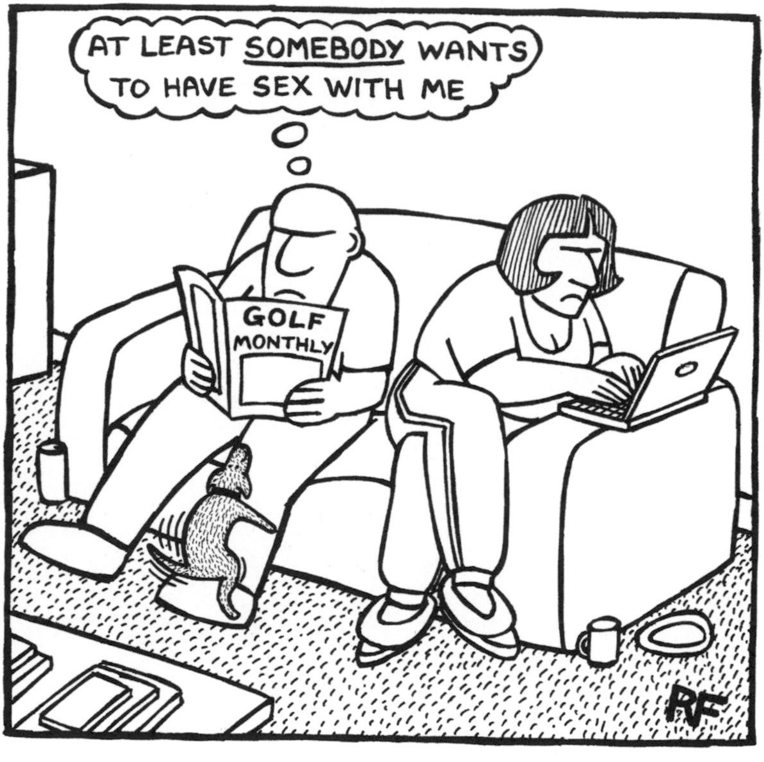
AT LEAST SOMEBODY WANTS TO HAVE SEX WITH ME
GOLF MONTHLY
RF

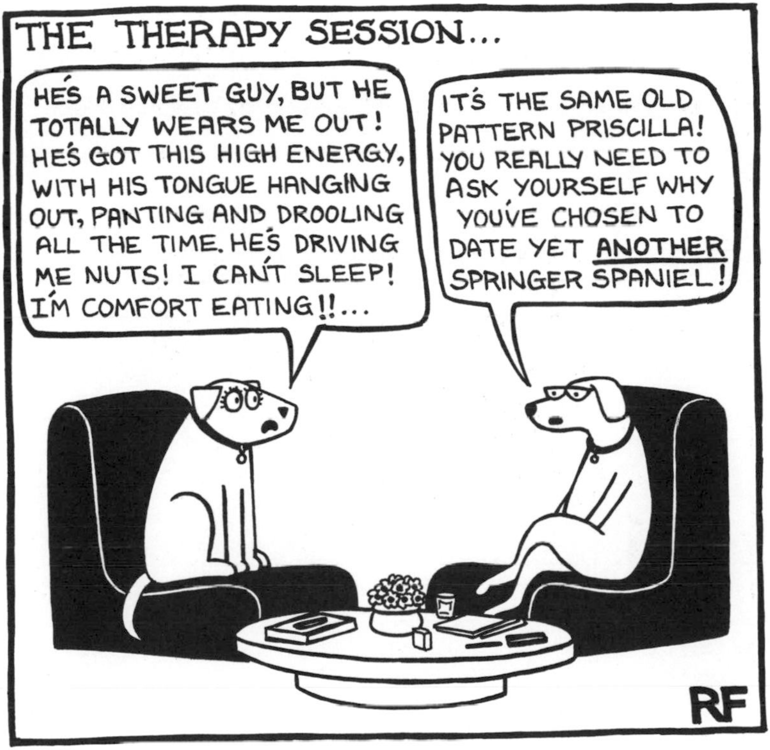
THE THERAPY SESSION...
HE'S A SWEET GUY, BUT HE TOTALLY WEARS ME OUT! HE'S GOT THIS HIGH ENERGY, WITH HIS TONGUE HANGING OUT, PANTING AND DROOLING ALL THE TIME. HE'S DRIVING ME NUTS! I CAN'T SLEEP! I'M COMFORT EATING!!...
IT'S THE SAME OLD PATTERN PRISCILLA! YOU REALLY NEED TO ASK YOURSELF WHY YOU'VE CHOSEN TO DATE YET ANOTHER SPRINGER SPANIEL!
RF

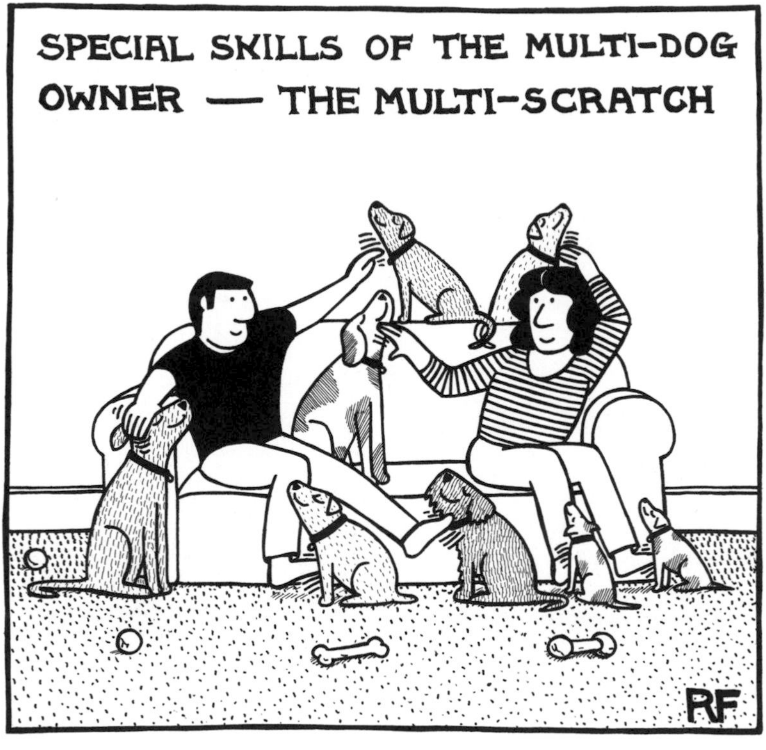
SPECIAL SKILLS OF THE MULTI-DOG OWNER — THE MULTI-SCRATCH
RF

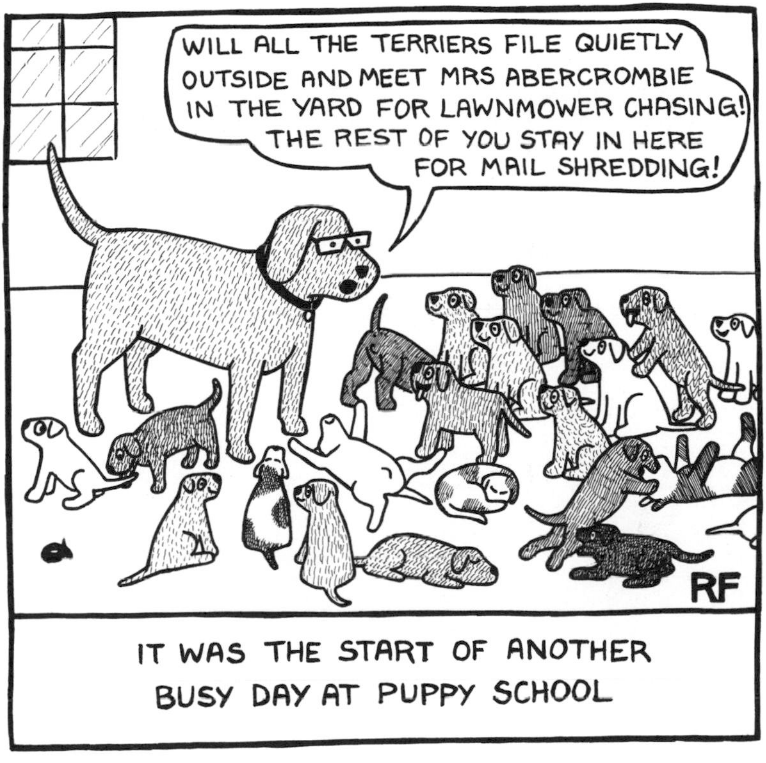
WILL ALL THE TERRIERS FILE QUIETLY OUTSIDE AND MEET MRS ABERCROMBIE IN THE YARD FOR LAWNMOWER CHASING! THE REST OF YOU STAY IN HERE FOR MAIL SHREDDING!
RF

IT WAS THE START OF ANOTHER BUSY DAY AT PUPPY SCHOOL

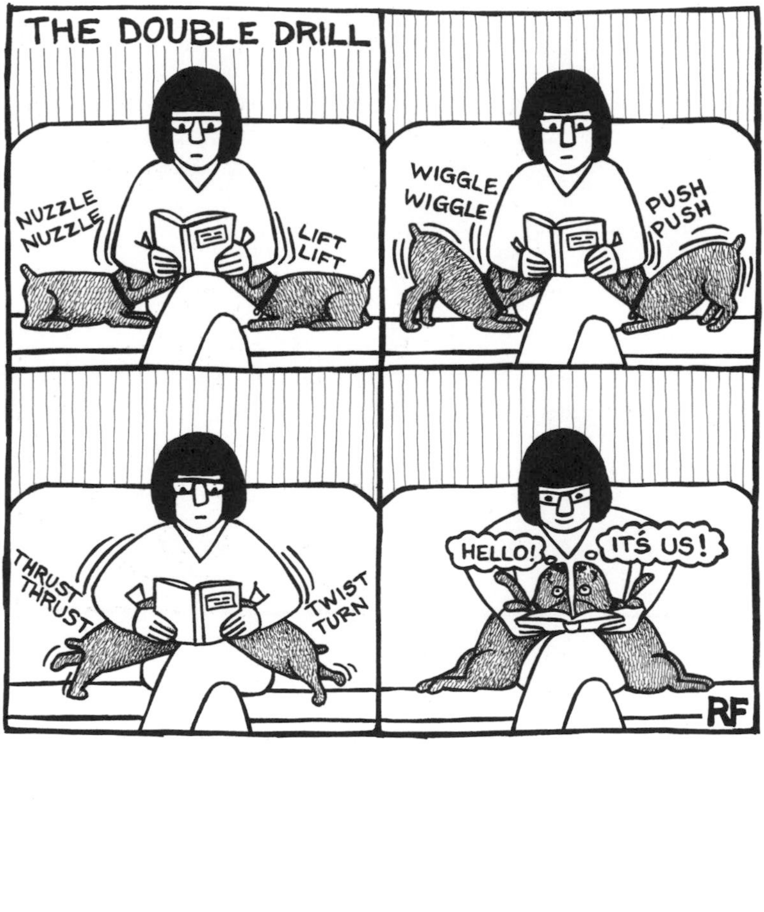
THE DOUBLE DRILL
NUZZLE NUZZLE
LIFT LIFT
WIGGLE WIGGLE
PUSH PUSH
THRUST THRUST
TWIST TURN
HELLO!
IT'S US!
RF

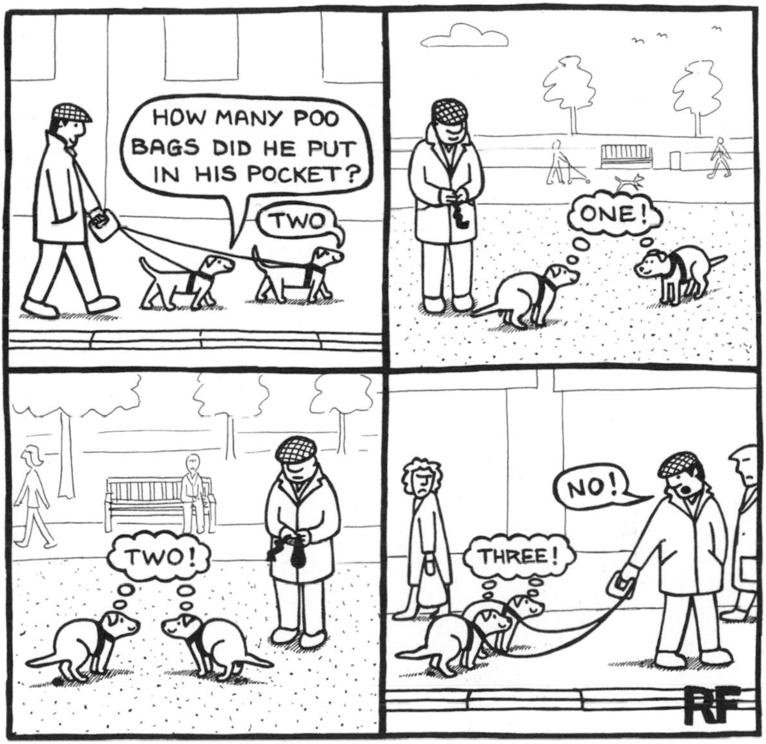
HOW MANY POO BAGS DID HE PUT IN HIS POCKET?
TWO
ONE!
TWO!
THREE!
NO!
RF

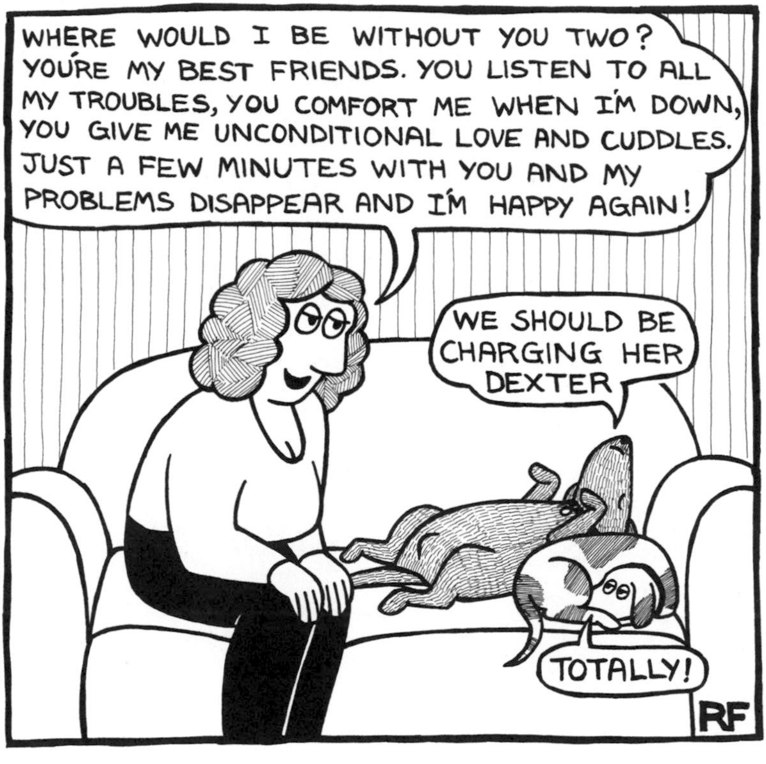
WHERE WOULD I BE WITHOUT YOU TWO? YOU'RE MY BEST FRIENDS. YOU LISTEN TO ALL MY TROUBLES, YOU COMFORT ME WHEN I'M DOWN, YOU GIVE ME UNCONDITIONAL LOVE AND CUDDLES. JUST A FEW MINUTES WITH YOU AND MY PROBLEMS DISAPPEAR AND I'M HAPPY AGAIN!
WE SHOULD BE CHARGING HER DEXTER
TOTALLY!
RF

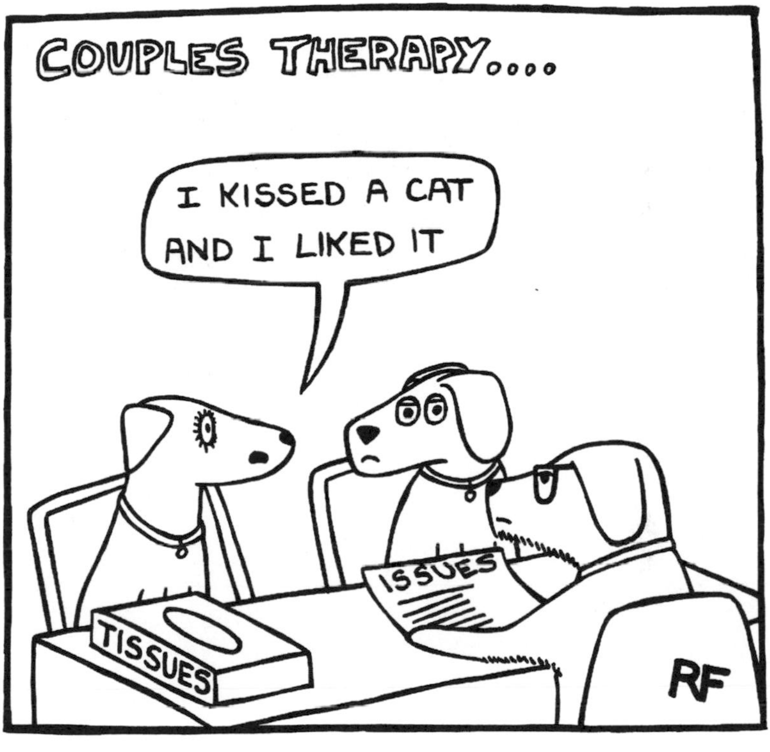
COUPLES THERAPY....
I KISSED A CAT AND I LIKED IT
ISSUES
TISSUES
RF

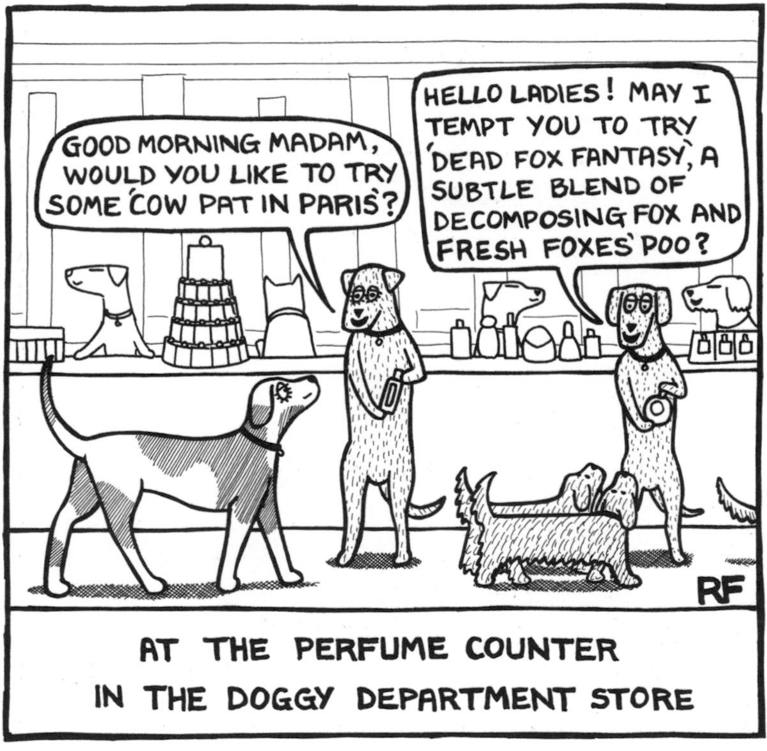
GOOD MORNING MADAM, WOULD YOU LIKE TO TRY SOME 'COW PAT IN PARIS'?
HELLO LADIES! MAY I TEMPT YOU TO TRY 'DEAD FOX FANTASY', A SUBTLE BLEND OF DECOMPOSING FOX AND FRESH FOXES' POO?
RF

AT THE PERFUME COUNTER
IN THE DOGGY DEPARTMENT STORE

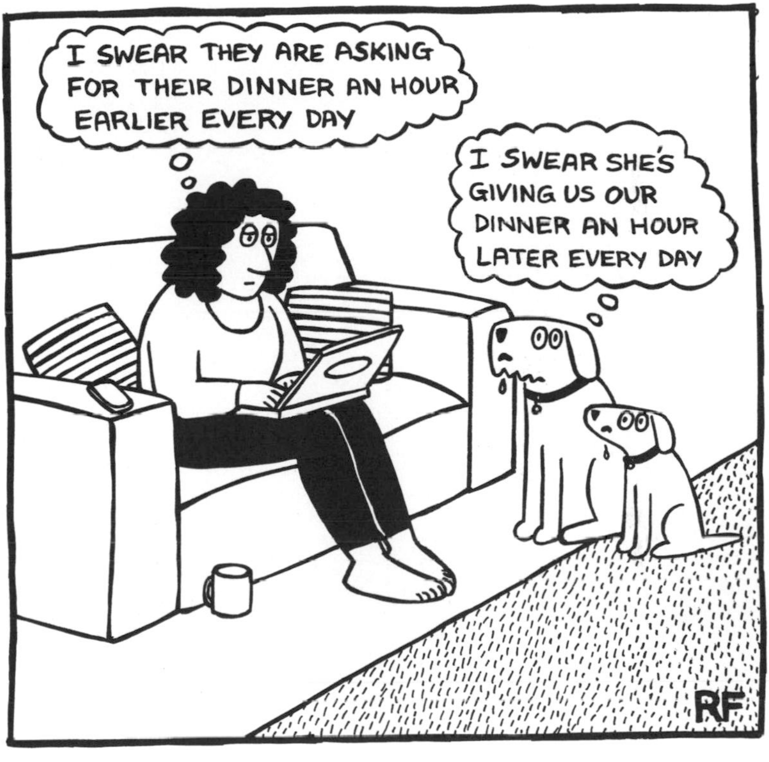
I SWEAR THEY ARE ASKING FOR THEIR DINNER AN HOUR EARLIER EVERY DAY
I SWEAR SHE'S GIVING US OUR DINNER AN HOUR LATER EVERY DAY
RF

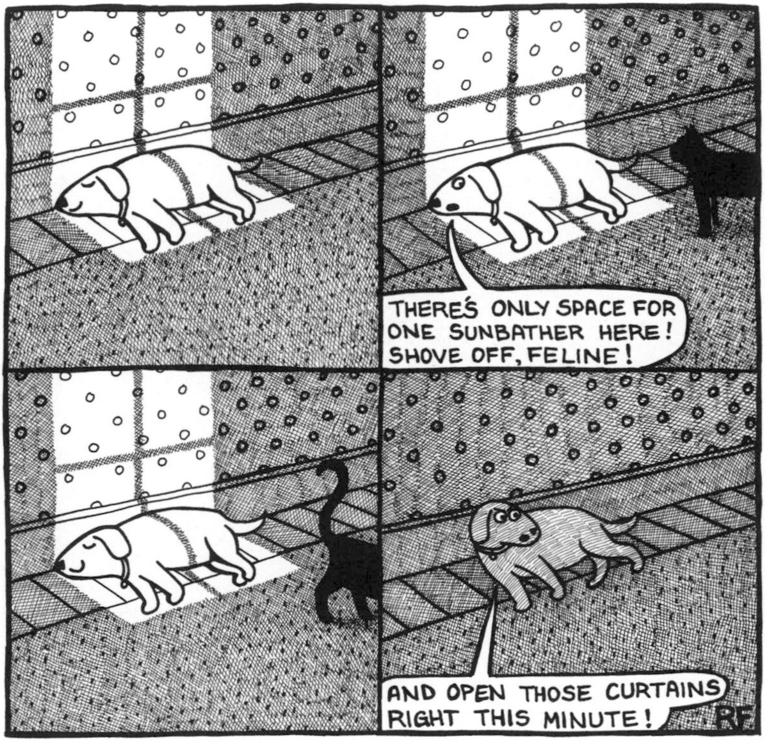
THERE'S ONLY SPACE FOR ONE SUNBATHER HERE! SHOVE OFF, FELINE!
AND OPEN THOSE CURTAINS RIGHT THIS MINUTE!
RF

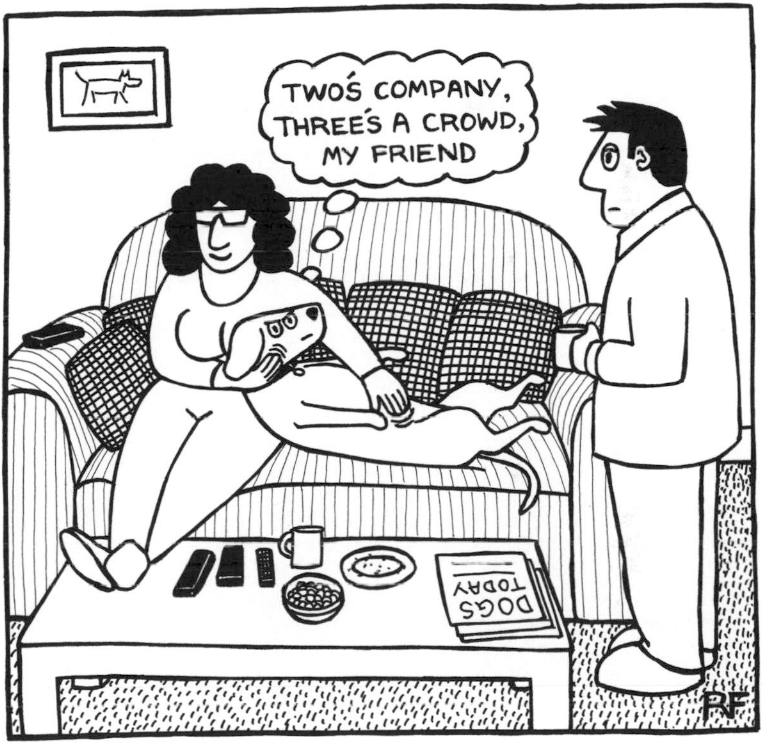
TWO'S COMPANY, THREE'S A CROWD, MY FRIEND
DOGS TODAY
RF

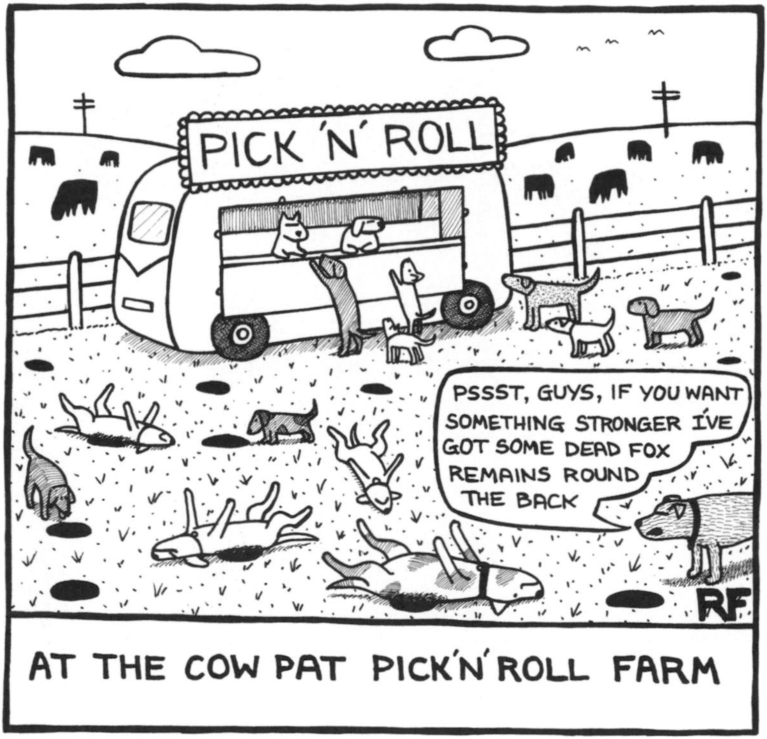
PICK 'N' ROLL
PSSST, GUYS, IF YOU WANT SOMETHING STRONGER I'VE GOT SOME DEAD FOX REMAINS ROUND THE BACK
RF

AT THE COW PAT PICK'N'ROLL FARM

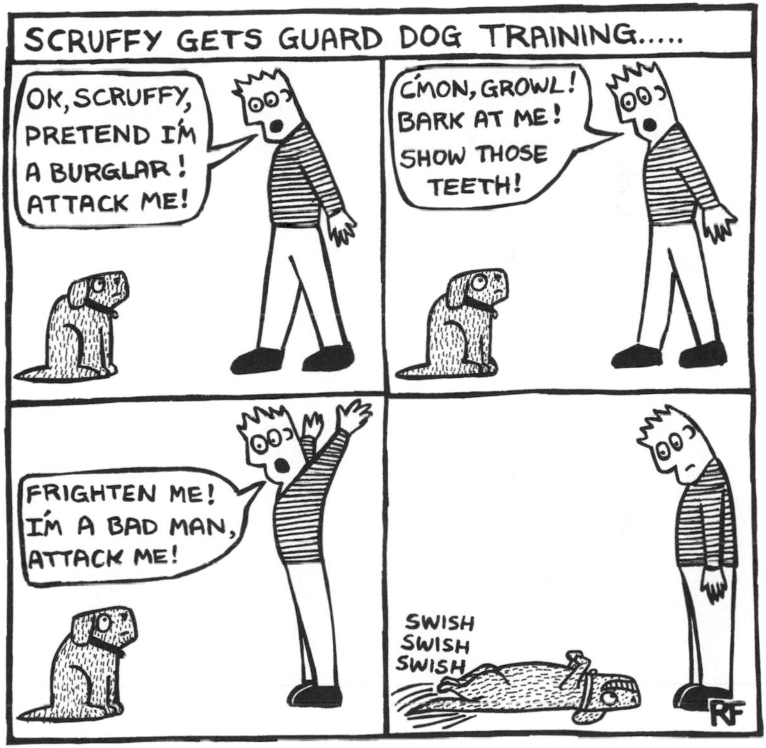
SCRUFFY GETS GUARD DOG TRAINING.....
OK, SCRUFFY, PRETEND I'M A BURGLAR! ATTACK ME!
C'MON, GROWL! BARK AT ME! SHOW THOSE TEETH!
FRIGHTEN ME! I'M A BAD MAN, ATTACK ME!
SWISH SWISH SWISH
RF

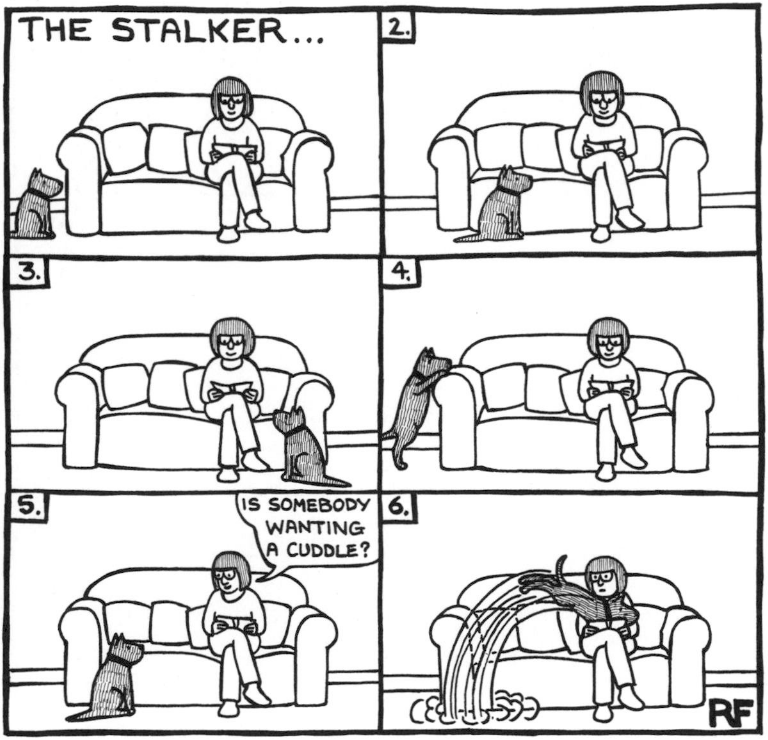
THE STALKER...
2.
3.
4.
5.
IS SOMEBODY WANTING A CUDDLE?
6.
RF

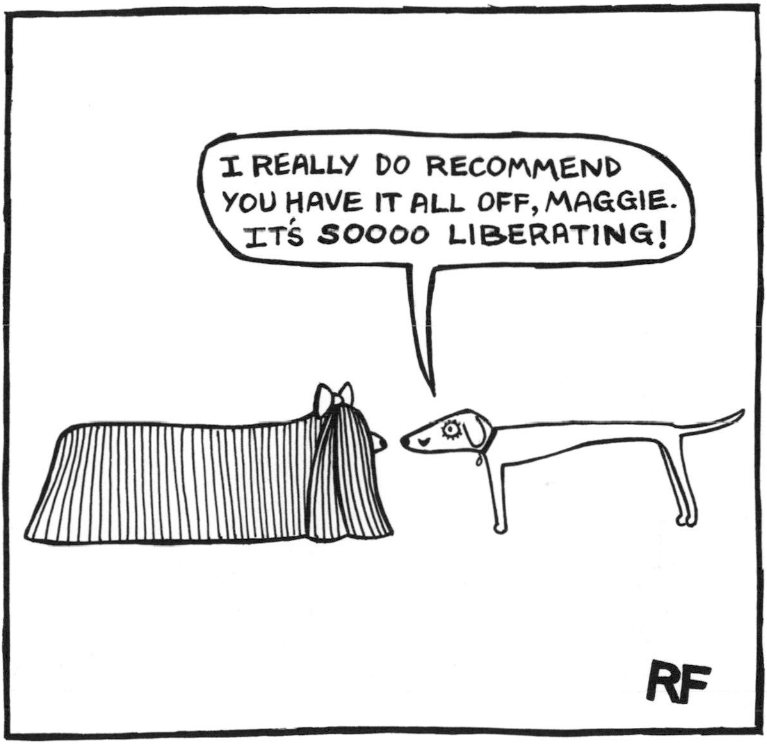
I REALLY DO RECOMMEND YOU HAVE IT ALL OFF, MAGGIE. IT'S SOOOO LIBERATING!
RF

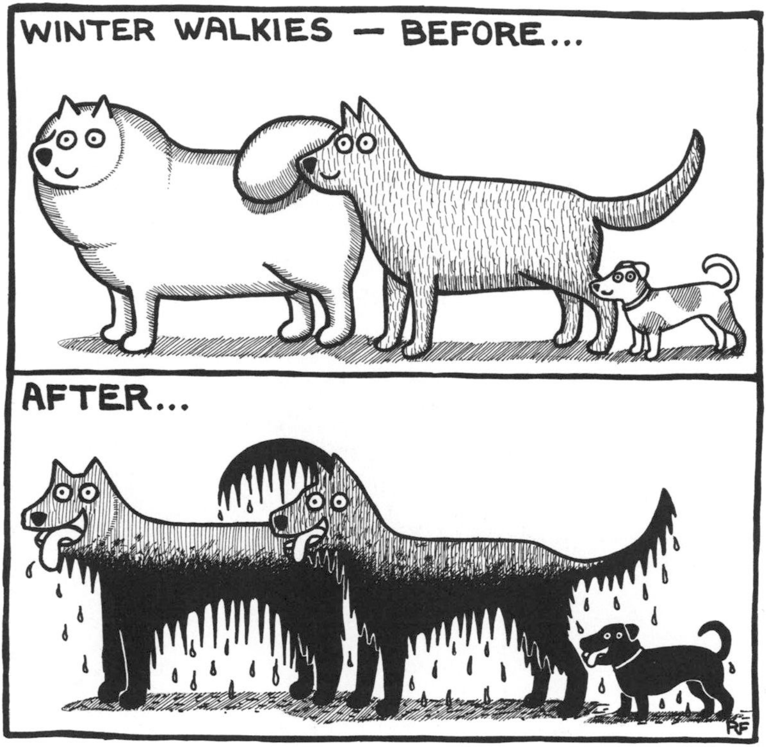
WINTER WALKIES — BEFORE...
AFTER...
RF

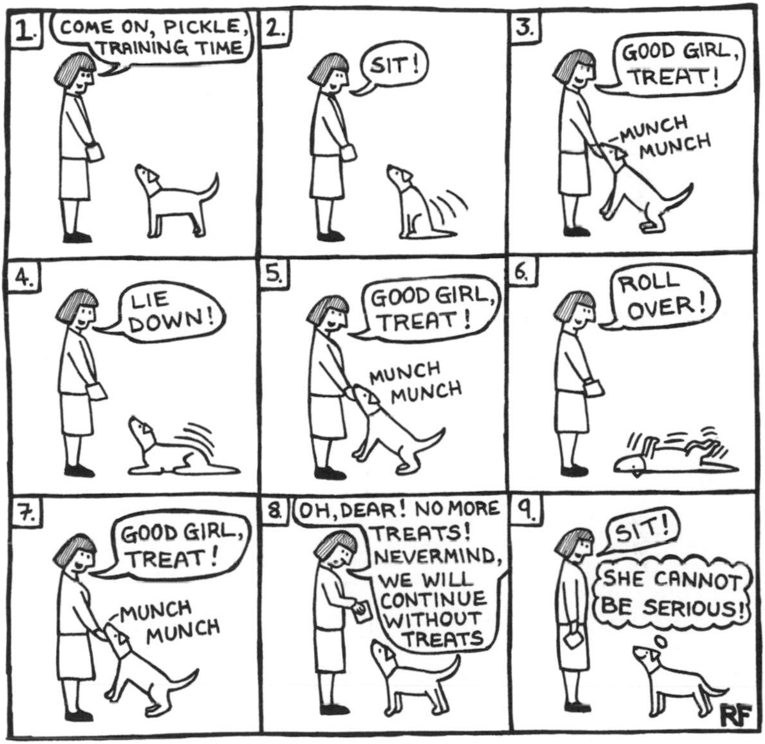
1.
COME ON, PICKLE, TRAINING TIME
2.
SIT!
3.
GOOD GIRL, TREAT!
MUNCH MUNCH
4.
LIE DOWN!
5.
GOOD GIRL, TREAT!
MUNCH MUNCH
6.
ROLL OVER!
7.
GOOD GIRL, TREAT!
MUNCH MUNCH
8.
OH, DEAR! NO MORE TREATS! NEVERMIND, WE WILL CONTINUE WITHOUT TREATS
9.
SIT!
SHE CANNOT BE SERIOUS!
RF

AT THE DOGGY LIBRARY...

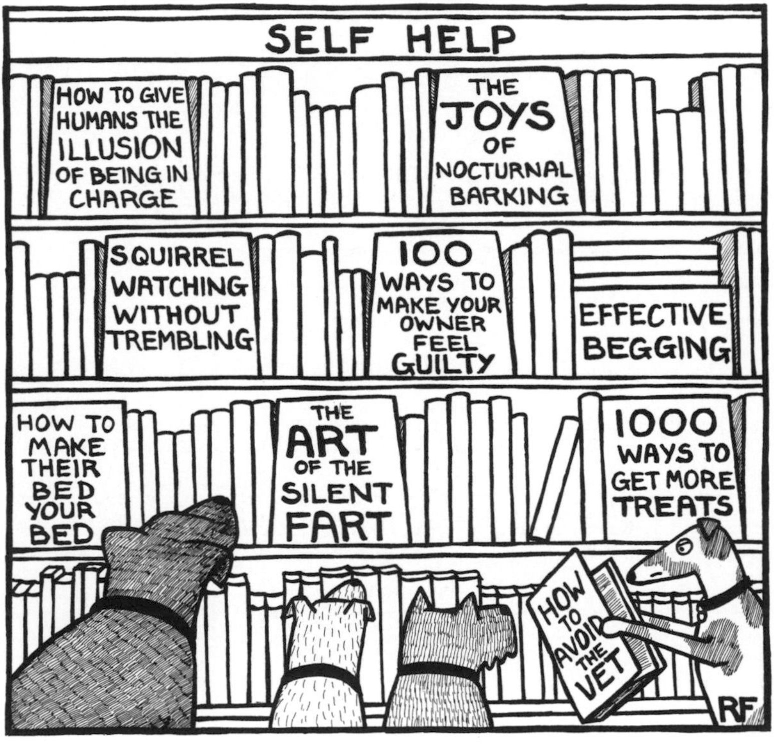
SELF HELP
HOW TO GIVE HUMANS THE ILLUSION OF BEING IN CHARGE
THE JOYS OF NOCTURNAL BARKING
SQUIRREL WATCHING WITHOUT TREMBLING
100 WAYS TO MAKE YOUR OWNER FEEL GUILTY
EFFECTIVE BEGGING
HOW TO MAKE THEIR BED YOUR BED
THE ART OF THE SILENT FART
1000 WAYS TO GET MORE TREATS
HOW TO AVOID THE VET
RF

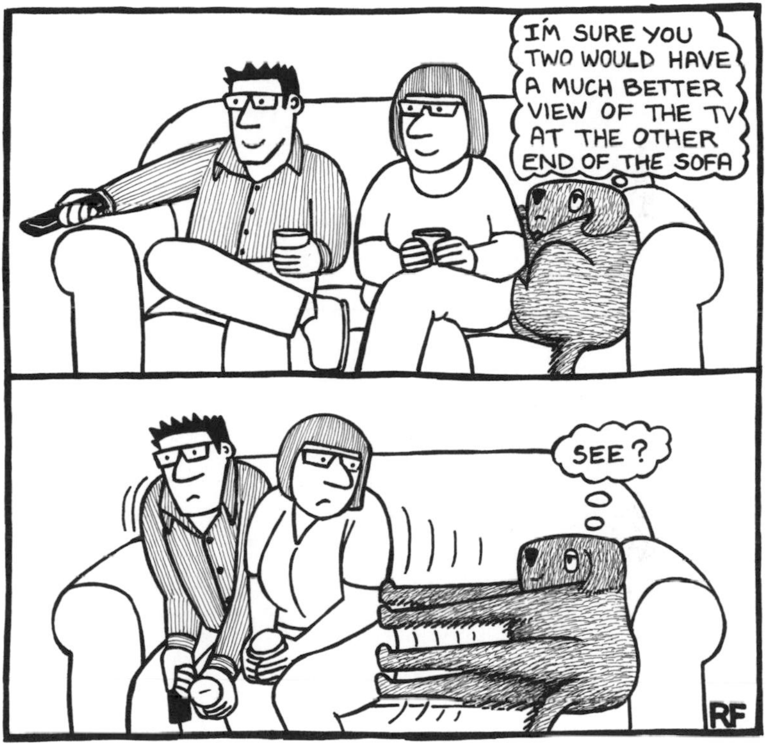
I'M SURE YOU TWO WOULD HAVE A MUCH BETTER VIEW OF THE TV AT THE OTHER END OF THE SOFA
SEE?
RF

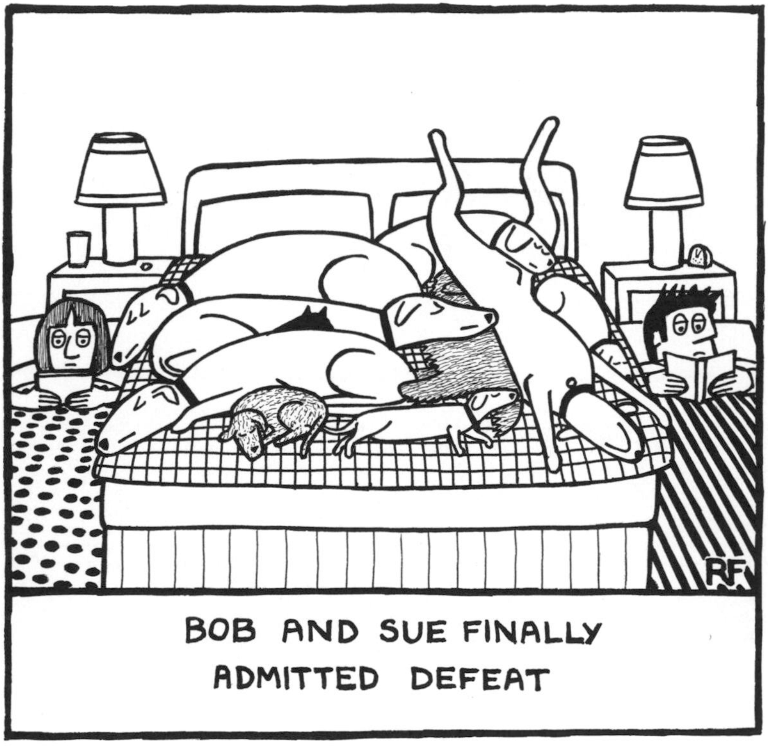
RF

BOB AND SUE FINALLY
ADMITTED DEFEAT

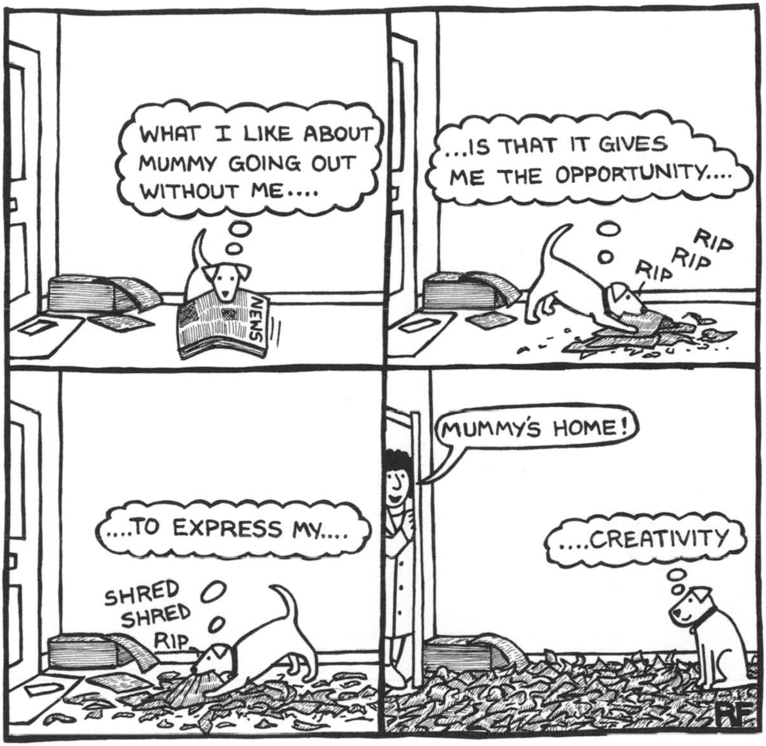
WHAT I LIKE ABOUT MUMMY GOING OUT WITHOUT ME....
NEWS
...IS THAT IT GIVES ME THE OPPORTUNITY....
RIP
RIP
RIP
....TO EXPRESS MY....
SHRED
SHRED
RIP
MUMMY'S HOME!
....CREATIVITY
RF

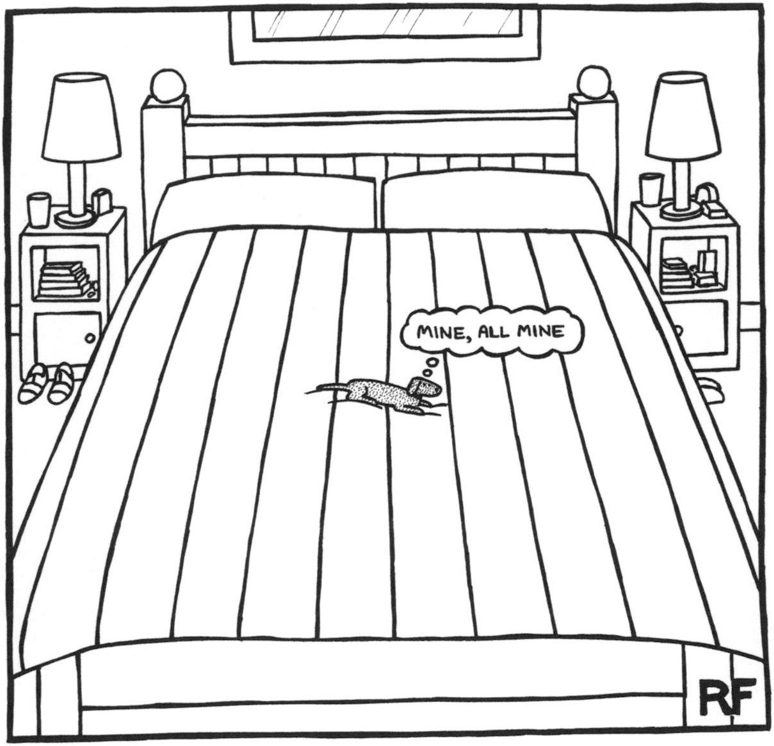
MINE, ALL MINE
RF

About the author

Rupert Fawcett became a professional cartoonist almost by accident when in 1989, whilst doodling, he drew a bald man in braces and carpet slippers and called him Fred. The Fred cartoons went on to be syndicated in the *Mail on Sunday* and published in several books. To date more than 9 million Fred greetings cards have been sold in the UK, Australia and New Zealand. Off The Leash is his latest creation.

www.rupertfawcettcartoons.com
www.facebook.com/OffTheLeashDailyDogCartoons